T0271421

Sustainable Governance in B Corps

This book aims to develop the theme of non-financial reporting and the necessity of pursuing sustainable development with particular reference to Benefit Corporations and Certified B Corps. The research offers a systematic and exploratory analysis, with the goal of developing a conceptual framework for supporting companies in the achievement of sustainable governance in line with the United Nations' guidelines for sustainable development. The first chapter reviews the relevant literature and analyzes the concept of sustainable development, focusing on the United Nations' policies and SDGs. Chapter 2 reviews the relevant literature on corporate social responsibility, describing its evolution from its birth during the Industrial Revolution through to the present day. Chapter 3 focuses on non-financial reporting and emphasizes the need to establish effective social communication with stakeholders that includes environmental, social, and governance (ESG) aspects. Chapter 4 explores the value of Benefit Corporations and Certified B Corps, which are companies that have adopted an innovative business model that combines the need for both corporate social responsibility and profitability. Finally, the last chapter uses examples of Italian fashion B Corps to illustrate how such companies make decisions based on CSR.

Patrizia Gazzola, associate professor, Department of Economics, University of Insubria, Varese, Italy.

Matteo Ferioli, research fellow, Department of Economics, University of Insubria, Varese, Italy.

Routledge Focus on Business and Management

The fields of business and management have grown exponentially as areas of research and education. This growth presents challenges for readers trying to keep up with the latest important insights. *Routledge Focus on Business and Management* presents small books on big topics and how they intersect with the world of business research.

Individually, each title in the series provides coverage of a key academic topic, whilst collectively, the series forms a comprehensive collection across the business disciplines.

Knowledge Management and AI in Society 5.0
Manlio Del Giudice, Veronica Scuotto and Armando Papa

The Logistics Audit
Methods, Organization and Practice
Piotr Buła and Bartosz Niedzielski

Women's Social Entrepreneurship
Case Studies from the United Kingdom
Panagiotis Kyriakopoulos

Business Schools post-Covid-19
A Blueprint for Survival
Andreas Kaplan

Sustainable Governance in B Corps
Non-Financial Reporting for Sustainable Development
Patrizia Gazzola and Matteo Ferioli

For more information about this series, please visit: www.routledge.com/Routledge-Focus-on-Business-and-Management/book-series/FBM

Sustainable Governance in B Corps

Non-Financial Reporting for Sustainable Development

**Patrizia Gazzola and
Matteo Ferioli**

Routledge
Taylor & Francis Group

NEW YORK AND LONDON

First published 2024
by Routledge
605 Third Avenue, New York, NY 10158

and by Routledge
4 Park Square, Milton Park, Abingdon, Oxon, OX14 4RN

Routledge is an imprint of the Taylor & Francis Group, an informa business

© 2024 Patrizia Gazzola and Matteo Ferioli

ISBN: 978-1-032-47094-8 (hbk)
ISBN: 978-1-032-48324-5 (pbk)
ISBN: 978-1-003-38847-0 (ebk)

DOI: 10.4324/9781003388470

Typeset in Times New Roman
by MPS Limited, Dehradun

Contents

Introduction

Today's global business environment is highly dynamic and ever-changing, which puts pressure on organizations to find ways to exploit opportunities to stay competitive and overcome risks. A lack of sustainable governance exposes companies to social and environmental threats that jeopardize their sustainability and individual well-being, with negative consequences for their profitability. In this context, organizations need to adopt sustainable governance and develop a resilient capacity that allows them to adequately react to unforeseen events in order to survive in the long term and promote future success. This book explores the role of non-financial reporting and argues that companies need to pursue sustainable development in line with the European Union's directive. Specifically, the book explains how companies can achieve sustainable environmental, social, and governance (ESG) performance.

Corporate social responsibility (CSR) has become the new imperative for organizations to be successful and maintain a long-term competitive advantage because it allows them to differentiate their products from competitors and eases financial constraints and market access. Therefore, it has become a necessity to stay relevant in the market and compete in the long term by pursuing the Sustainable Development Goals (SDGs) defined by the United Nations General Assembly. Over the years, stakeholders have become increasingly interested in knowing what kind of impact companies have on society and on the environment and what activities companies undertake to sustain living conditions and opportunities for future generations. Therefore, they have become increasingly attentive to how companies pursue their corporate purpose, and they have started requiring more information about companies' activities in this regard. Thus, it has become critical that companies carry out internal and external analyses to understand their ESG impacts. To this end, social communication and non-financial reporting have assumed an increasingly important role over the years,

DOI: 10.4324/9781003388470-1

especially for sustainable companies such as B Corps. Thanks to non-financial reporting, companies and stakeholders can evaluate performance from an internal and external point of view. The internal analysis mainly refers to governance and policies regarding internal processes, materiality, and the resulting impacts, while external analysis involves relations with all stakeholders. The non-financial statement (NFS) and the integrated report are effective social communication tools because they allow companies and stakeholders to evaluate financial and sustainability performance through the disclosure of appropriate information on financial, environmental, social, and governance performance. These aspects are particularly relevant to B Corps because they have an innovative business model that enables them to be profitable while undertaking corporate social responsibility activities. B Corps have higher standards of purpose, responsibility, and transparency than traditional companies and use the integrated report to meet the needs of efficiency and social communication. Although B Corps are innovative companies, they have received limited coverage in the scholarly literature. Therefore, this book aims to deepen our field's understanding of this topic and provide case studies as exemplars for future application.

The book begins by reviewing the relevant literature about the importance of sustainable development, corporate social responsibility, and non-financial reporting. It shows why it is necessary to pursue sustainable development with sustainable governance and aims to investigate how truly sustainable organizations, such as B Corps, use non-financial reporting to increase the efficiency of their resources and the effectiveness of their social communication.

Chapter 1 defines the concept of sustainable development, focusing on United Nations' policies and SDGs. Over the years, the concept of sustainability has evolved and its scope has broadened to embrace all categories of stakeholders. Today, it is fundamental for organizations' long-term survival that they develop a system of common goals that enable all parts of society to grow in a more sustainable direction. To do this, it is necessary to engage in dialogue with stakeholders. Sustainable development needs a plan that meets the needs of current generations while preserving resources for future generations. Social communication has also become increasingly important for organizations, especially following the introduction of Directive 2014/95/EU of the European Parliament and the Council and Legislative Decree 254/2016.

Chapter 2 reviews the relevant literature on the concept of corporate social responsibility, describing its evolution from its birth during the Industrial Revolution through the present day. It defines CSR's primary characteristics and illustrates how CSR became the new imperative for companies to compete and succeed in the long term. The chapter describes the historical evolution of CSR by focusing on the main theories and events that transformed it from a voluntary choice to a necessity for long-term organizational survival, which is especially true in the post-pandemic period. CSR requires new business models to address sustainability issues and meet social needs.

Chapter 3 focuses on non-financial reporting as a tool for internal and external analyses and emphasizes the need for companies to establish effective social communication with stakeholders that includes environmental, social, and governance (ESG) aspects. The chapter introduces ESG principles and explores the value of organization's disclosing their non-financial information through an integrated report, which is a document that provides space for the disclosure of financial, governance, and sustainability performance information.

Chapter 4 explores Benefit Corporations and Certified B Corps, which are companies that have adopted an innovative business model that combines the need for corporate social responsibility and profitability. It clarifies the differences between these two categories of companies and highlights their common goal of contributing to the well-being of society and the environment. B Corps have higher standards of transparency than traditional corporations and communicate effectively with stakeholders through their NFS (or sustainability report). However, in recent years, many organizations are increasingly disclosing financial and non-financial information through an integrated report, thus moving from the concept of separate thinking toward integrated thinking. This chapter illustrates the different social communication standards imposed by law and B Lab on Benefit Corporations and Certified B Corps.

Chapter 5 introduces the case study of the Italian fashion industry, which has been accused of posing sustainability challenges by exploiting marketing strategies that promote consumerism. Increased stakeholder's attention to social and environmental sustainability created the need for companies to adopt ethical business practices. Therefore, many fashion companies adopted standards and codes of conduct to manage their impacts on society and the environment. Furthermore, Italian fashion companies are increasingly adopting the B Corps' innovative business model to achieve sustainable development and the United Nations' SDGs. However, a comprehensive plan to address sustainability and create long-term shared value is needed.

The conclusion emphasizes that stakeholders are not only interested in financial performance but they increasingly require non-financial information as well. To this end, the integrated report is the ideal tool to increase the effectiveness of social communication and the efficiency of resources because it promotes the performance of internal and external analyses of an organization's financial, social, environmental, and governance aspects.

1 Sustainable development and the United Nations' Sustainable Development Goals

1.1 Sustainable development

The literature review on sustainable development reveals the lack of a complete theoretical framework for fully understanding this complex issue (Jabareen, 2004). The literature presents vague definitions of sustainable development and highlights a disagreement about what should be supported (Gow, 1992; Redclift, 1994; Sachs, 1999; Qizilbash, 2001). The concept of sustainable development remains confusing, as it is not clearly defined in terms of emotional commitment and the varying definitions present contradictions (Redclift, 1987, 1993; Solow, 1992). For this reason, there is no unanimous agreement in the literature on how it should be implemented in practice (Berke & Conroy, 2000). Although sustainable development has been studied for years, it still requires elaboration (Beatley et al. 1998). Indeed, it remains "symbolic rhetoric with competing interests" used to support policy agendas rather than serve as a basis for policy development (Andrews, 1997, p. 19).

The sustainable development concept refers to long-term development that includes economic aspects, as well as other elements, including education, health, and quality of life. An example of a measure of sustainable development is the United Nations' Human Development Index (HDI). HDI measures a country's success relative to other countries and combines measures of sub-goals such as education, life expectancy, and gross domestic product. The most widely used definition of sustainable development is that found in the 1987 World Commission on Environment and Development (WCED) report on North–South relations and the global environmental problem. The WCED states that sustainable development meets the needs of present generations without compromising the ability to meet the needs of future ones. Although the definition is broad, it is possible to assert that sustainable development enables economic progress while preserving the long-term value of the environment and society. Furthermore, it "provides a framework for the integration of environmental policies and development strategies"

DOI: 10.4324/9781003388470-2

(UN General Assembly, 1987). Therefore, it suggests that environmental and social sustainability and economic development are related. The challenge of conserving resources for future generations is the characteristic that distinguishes sustainable development policy from traditional environmental policy. The goal of sustainable development is the long-term stability of society, the economy, and the environment, and this is possible only by integrating social, economic, and environmental concerns into business strategies across territories, sectors, and generations (Emas, 2015). It requires considering these concerns during all decision-making processes to enable development that is truly sustainable. This ambition distinguishes sustainability from other forms of policy.

Jabareen (2008) has identified seven distinct concepts that make up the concept of sustainability:

1 *Ethical paradox*: Sustainability is seen as a characteristic of a process that can be maintained over the long term. However, development implies environmental modification and requires a significant intervention in nature, which depletes natural resources.
2 *Natural capital stock*: The term natural capital is "the stock of all environmental and natural resources, from oil on land to soil and groundwater quality, from fish stocks in the ocean to the globe's ability to recycle and absorb carbon" (Pearce & Turner, 1989; Pearce et al., 2013, p. 1).
3 *Equity*: The concept of equity includes all social aspects of the sustainable development concept (i.e., equal development rights; environmental, social, and economic justice; social equity; quality of life; equitable distribution economics; freedom; public participation; democracy; and empowerment). The social dimension is essential for society to become environmentally or economically sustainable in the long run (Haughton, 1999). Agyeman et al. (2002) argue that dispossession and environmental degradation are related to the issues of equity, rights, social justice, and people's quality of life. For this reason, a sustainable society satisfies social needs and considers equity, well-being, and economic opportunities without forgetting the environmental limits imposed by ecosystems.
4 *Eco-form*: Sustainability requires attention to ecological design for the definition of urban forms that allow buildings to function sustainably.
5 *Integrative management*: To achieve sustainability and ecological integrity, it is necessary to use an integrated and holistic management approach. Therefore, it is crucial to consider the needs of society, economic growth, and environmental protection in an integrated way.
6 *Utopianism*: The utopian concept imagines a perfect society where human habitats (i.e., cities, communities, regions, and the globe) are

based on the concept of sustainable development. It sees the future in terms of new values and forms where people live and thrive in harmony with nature without any abuses or deficiencies.

7 *Political global agenda*: This concept has been reconstructed and inspired by the ideas of sustainable development of the 1990s, where the central adage of environmental policies was globalized. Sustainable development began as a political statement that took an ethical position with theoretical and practical implications (Hatfield Dodds, 2000). It aims to tackle global and unified environmental and development problems and their causes to provide the tools and resources necessary to address deforestation, population growth, climate change, biodiversity loss, diseases, and poverty.

This last point reflects the need for a single guide that unites all parts of society on a global level. For this reason, the European Union has developed the Sustainable Development Goals (SDGs).

1.2 Sustainable revolution

Edwards (2005) defines this period of change as "sustainable revolution," which he identifies based on the following specific characteristics:

- *Complexity*: Contemporary institutions, cultures, and communications technologies form the foundation of our complex and developed world. The sustainable revolution takes place in this world.
- *Number of stakeholders*: It is necessary to consider the different subjects that are involved.
- *Stakeholder expectations*: In our contemporary world, people have very high expectations, not only in terms of consumption but also in terms of lifestyles, health, and well-being. This is not only particular to the developed world; developing countries are also raising their expectations.
- *Public interest issues*: General welfare, justice, and human rights are becoming increasingly important.
- *Globalization of markets and information technologies*: In our complex contemporary world, communication systems are increasingly faster and more available (Mashado des Johansson & Burns, 2012).

There is an important connection between all of these characteristics. They cannot be considered separately to determine the direct influence of every sustainable factor because some are direct consequences of others. For example, it is evident that globalization is very connected to rapid technological advances and competition among businesses, which, in turn, leads companies to pursue growth through globalization.

The globalization of markets (Scherer & Palazzo, 2008) has allowed companies to search for new opportunities for expansion and profit abroad. In the contemporary world market, the rapid progress of technologies has reduced the distances between different countries, leading to an increase in globalization. Such technologies allow individuals and non-profit organizations (NPO) all over the world to be in contact with and monitor business behavior. Indeed, if a company creates negative impacts on the environment and does not take human rights into consideration, the fact can quickly go around the world thanks to effective and increasingly global media.

Negative comments about products and services that are posted on forums, blogs, etc. are quickly shared with a much wider audience via social media. This has direct impacts on the behavior of companies. Multinationals are now more concerned about sustainability because they need to avoid scandals. Consumers and NGOs can easily boycott a company thanks to the speed of information and the ease of aggregation. Some multinationals have an office open 24 hours a day to monitor their consumers' social media, thus facilitating the diffusion of ideas of sustainability. They accelerate innovation rates and the application of sustainable development by connecting people and every kind of organization to be invested in improving sustainability.

Moreover, global competition generates new opportunities. If consumers want to report an organization that is dangerous to the population's health or the environment, there are always NPOs or business competitors who are ready to support them. Sustainability represents a critical source of competitive advantage. Specifically, globalization has led to a very marked increase in competition. Global competition places particular pressure on businesses, especially multinationals, to evaluate not only their sustainability practices but also the sustainability of their supply chain.

Nonprofit organizations continue to take on a more significant role by harnessing the media and the Internet to increase their collective control and activism around business behavior. For instance, the great pollution scandals have garnered lots of attention for sustainable development and increased social awareness about the existence of these problems. The well-known NPO Greenpeace is very active with campaigns and actions that are often very powerful and have been effective at influencing critical business decisions. Among others, we can point out the recent Greenpeace campaign against the use of plastic and the problems with palm oil.

Consumer demand is increasing due to the rise in the world's population, putting pressure on our scarce natural resources. While industrialization has created opportunities for new jobs, it has simultaneously exploited a great number of resources, with deforestation being an excellent example of the damage such exploitation renders. Globalization and the rapid spread of information have resulted in people being more informed of the environmental and social implications of their daily decisions, especially the environmental and ethical aspects. Sustainability initiatives continue to grow and have already reached the tens of thousands. Their development, however, takes place in the context of existing social structures, with the power configurations already outlined and interests already established. Moreover, investors prefer to invest in companies that behave responsibly. When making investment decisions, they consider not only the profit potential but also a company's commitment to sustainability. In this way, they put pressure on businesses to commit to sustainability. This is confirmed by the establishment of the FTSE4Good Index and Dow Jones Sustainability World Index (DJSI World). For many businesses, being included in these indexes is an important public recognition of their corporate virtue.

1.3 The SDGs for the biosphere, society, and the economy

In the last decade, the necessity of developing a system of common goals to enable all parts of society to work in a common and more sustainable direction has gained increasing attention. The objectives of the UN 2030 Agenda are very clear. They are concerned with the looming "evils" of modernity, which seriously jeopardize future development and the well-being of future generations. One of the Agenda's mottos is "The future we don't want," which denounces the level of unsustainability reached in various areas of our collective life, both globally and locally. Thus, the United Nations (UN) developed the SDGs 2030 with the aim of changing the dominant paradigm and demonstrating the unsustainability of the current growth model by emphasizing the need for an integrated vision of the various dimensions of development. In fact, it is believed that, in order to be sustainable and preserve the planet for future generations from ecological, social, and civil points of view, development must be integrated with economic growth, environmental protection, and human and social rights.

Human activity has a negative and threatening impact on the world's ecosystems. Greenhouse gas emissions, increasing environmental pollution, fossil resource depletion, and groundwater pollution have led to continuous climate change (Italia, 2019). Moreover, advances in the fight against poverty and hunger and the growing need for sustainable development for the whole world led to the development of the SDGs (Sachs, 2012). The SDGs are 17 global goals developed by the United Nations to achieve a sustainable future worldwide by 2030. Some of the goals have no deadline for their achievement. The progress achieved and the remaining challenges for each country are assessed each year in the context of the High-Level Political Forum (HLPF) on Sustainable Development. These objectives encompass 169 targets, which can be both results and means of implementation (Desa, 2016). The essential characteristic of the goals is that they are universal, interconnected, and indivisible: even considering specific territorial characteristics, they are potentially applicable everywhere, at global, national, and local levels. The SDGs were developed in the Post-2015 Development Agenda[1] to succeed the Millennium Development Goals (MDGs)[2] in 2015 (Sachs, 2012). They are part of the United Nations resolution known as the 2030 Agenda. The SDGs represent the direction companies must take through 2030, committing themselves to respect and act in accordance with the required sustainability standards. The 2030 Agenda Goals differ from the previous ones, the Millennium Goals for 2015, in integrating the social, economic, and environmental dimensions, thereby definitively setting aside the idea that sustainability concerns only environmental issues.

The SDGs guide companies in formulating sustainable strategies and contributing to the well-being of society. By embracing the so-called triple bottom line (TBL)[3] approach to human well-being (Sachs, 2012; Gazzola et al., 2020a), they bring simultaneous social equity, economic, and environmental benefits. For example, the policies on health and education should also solve problems linked to climate issues (Gazzola et al., 2020a). Since SDGs reporting is becoming a widespread practice, it may become a reporting standard, which would make the sustainability reports more comparable (Gazzola et al., 2020a). The SDGs are as follows:

1 *No poverty*: End poverty in all its forms everywhere in all the forms.
2 *Zero hunger*: End hunger, achieve food security and improved nutrition and promote sustainable agriculture.
3 *Good health and well-being*: Ensure healthy lives and promote well-being for all at all ages.
4 *Quality education*: Ensure inclusive and equitable quality education and promote lifelong learning opportunities for all.
5 *Gender equality*: Achieve gender equality and empower all women and girls.
6 *Clean water and sanitation*: Ensure availability and sustainable management of water and sanitation for all.
7 *Affordable and clean energy*: Ensure access to affordable, reliable, sustainable, and modern energy for all.
8 *Decent work and economic growth*: Promote sustained, inclusive, and sustainable economic growth, full and productive employment, and decent work for all.

9 *Industry, innovation, and infrastructure*: Build resilient infrastructure, promote inclusive and sustainable industrialization, and foster innovation.

10 *Reducing inequality*: Reduce inequality within and among countries.

11 *Sustainable cities and communities*: Make cities and human settlements inclusive, safe, resilient, and sustainable.

12 *Responsible consumption and production*: Ensure sustainable consumption and production patterns.

13 *Climate action*: Take urgent action to combat climate change and its impacts.

14 *Life below water*: Conserve and sustainably use the oceans and seas, and marine resources for sustainable development.

15 *Life on land*: Protect, restore, and promote sustainable use of terrestrial ecosystems, sustainably manage forests, combat desertification, and halt and reverse land degradation and halt biodiversity loss.

16 *Peace, justice, and strong institutions*: Promote peaceful and inclusive societies for sustainable development, provide access to justice for all, and build effective, accountable, and inclusive institutions at all levels.

17 *Partnerships for the goals*: Strengthen the means of implementation and revitalize the Global Partnerships for Sustainable Development.

In accordance with the three dimensions of sustainable development outlined in the agenda, we can divide the SDGs into three macro groups: those relating to the biosphere (SDGs 6, 13, 14, and 15), to society (SDGs 8, 9, 10, and 12), or to the economy (SDGs 1, 2, 3, 4, 5, 7, 11, and 16). The goals related to the biosphere support those related to society, which in turn support the economic ones. The economy cannot be healthy if society is not healthy, and society cannot be healthy if the environment is not healthy. SDG 17 is applicable to each of them.

1.4 The 5P model

The United Nations' 2030 Agenda for Sustainable Development provides a global framework called the 5P Model, presented in *Transforming Our World: The 2030 Agenda for Sustainable Development* (United Nations, 2015). It reaffirms the principles and commits the 193 member states of the United Nations to implement sustainable development using a broader framework of action than the three pillars of environmental, economic, and social parameters indicated in the Brundtland Report (World Commission on Environment and Development, 1987).

The 5P Model considers the 17 SDGs as a framework rather than a group of individual goals and groups them into five categories: people, planet, prosperity, peace, and partnership (United Nations, 2015). Each category must be balanced and supported by all the others to achieve sustainable development.

1 People denotes a humane approach by focusing on poverty and hunger reduction in all shapes and sizes and ensuring that all human beings can fulfill their potential with dignity, equality, and a healthy environment. It is based on the principles of environmental and social justice that promote health and well-being. According to Morton et al. (2017), the category includes SDGs 1, 2, 3, 4, 5, and 6 and requires action to fight poverty and hunger and ensure access to quality education, clean water and sanitation, and health care, as well as clean energy and affordable prices. In this way, the first category aims to guarantee a dignified quality of life and to satisfy people's primary needs by ensuring the availability of all essential goods. For example, the well-being of society can be achieved by providing people with quality food and water, while, simultaneously, giving them access to education so that they can make the most of the economic and employment opportunities available in their country. However, Lawrence (2020) and Morton et al. (2017) point out that the people category does not explicitly address the influence of human motivations, beliefs, values, and worldviews that underlie the logic that frames the individual–society–environment interrelationships of the biosphere. Indeed, in a world of uncertain futures and unpredictable changes, interrelationships are defined by how groups of people and individuals think about supporting their livelihoods and their relationships with others (Morton et al., 2017).

2 Planet is focused on climate change and the loss of biodiversity and comprises SDGs 13, 14, and 15. It is dedicated to the evolution of global environmental conditions and to the protection of natural resources and the climate, as well as to supporting the needs of present and future generations. According to Arthur Dahl (1996), sustainable development is a voluntary process, and environmental concerns are constructs of human thought and behavior. The processes of consumption and production and the use of natural resources generate negative impacts on society and the environment, which reacts mainly through global warming and climate change. The harmful substances emitted into the atmosphere, such as carbon monoxide, nitrogen oxides, and hydrocarbons, produce significant risks to human health and food safety, as they pollute the water used for livestock and crops (Ferioli, 2022). These indirect negative impacts are reflected in the possibilities of global development and determine direct and indirect negative externalities for companies. For example, an unsustainable company could see its costs increase following the introduction of new

regulations aimed at reducing environmental and atmospheric pollution. This is particularly true in the more polluting sectors, such as fashion, energy, and transport (Ferioli, 2022). For this reason, it is essential to consider the SDGs in the formulation of strategies, bearing in mind that they are not short term, but require the investment of long-term commitment and resources to be achieved. In this way, it is possible to undertake sustainable actions that minimize the damage caused by climate impacts.

3 Prosperity refers to the means of subsistence provided by economic, social, and technological progress. This category encompasses goals number 7, 8, 9, 10, 11, and 12 and aims to ensure that everyone can enjoy a prosperous life and that economic, social, and technological progress occur in harmony with nature. The term prosperity means being able to enjoy a quality life through the realization of economic, social, and technological progress that is in harmony with the natural environment. The concept of prosperity is linked to inequality, which continues to characterize our society today and is present within companies. A lack of sincere and sufficient commitment to reduce inequalities, especially in income, consumption, access to health care, and education, continues to have significant consequences for life expectancy. To date, efforts to ensure decent working conditions have been slower than expected because the pandemic increased economic inequality. Furthermore, the achievement of social prosperity has been slowed down by economic, cultural, and social factors. Therefore, it is increasingly necessary to take action to achieve gender equality and reduce discrimination, such as ensuring equal working conditions for women and men. These efforts will first impact the workplace, narrowing the gender pay gap; subsequently, they will be reflected in society at large. In this way, it is possible to achieve the social and economic prosperity sought by the SDGs.

4 Peace promotes just and inclusive societies without violence, war, or a sense of insecurity. The category is based on SDG 16 and aims to promote peaceful, just, and inclusive societies. In this category, it is possible to group three areas of intervention, namely:

- Eliminate all forms of discrimination.
- Ensure legality and justice.
- Promote a non-violent and inclusive society.

Governments play a critical role in building and strengthening just and peaceful institutions. Therefore, it is necessary to ensure that everyone has equal access to justice and that it can be achieved by, for example, curbing corruption, protecting human rights, and supporting institutions that promote the rule of law. To achieve these sub-goals, the public and private sectors must work together globally. On the company side, employees should be able to expect working conditions that respect their rights. In addition, companies should collaborate with the public sector to put in place mechanisms aimed at curbing corruption.

5 Partnerships identifies the development of both business-to-business and public-private partnerships based on a spirit of solidarity and with the participation of all countries as necessary for a successful implementation of the United Nations Agenda for Sustainable Development. Partnerships require a fundamental change in values and were endorsed at the World Summit on Sustainable Development (United Nations, 2002).

1.5 The interconnections between the different goals

Morton et al.'s (2017) classification does not consider the interconnections between the different SDGs. However, the UN goals are interrelated, and some of them can be placed in more than one of the 5P categories. For this reason, the goals should be identified by systems and relational thinking (Werna & Lawrence, 2009; Elder et al., 2016). Elder et al. (2016) proposed a functional classification of the 17 SDGs based on the following six categories:

- Education (SDG 4)
- Governance (SDG 16)
- Resources (SDGs 2, 6, 7)
- Social goals (SDGs 1, 3, 4, 5, 10)
- Economy (SDGs 8, 9, 11, 12)
- Environment (SDGs 13, 14, 15)

SDG 17 is not part of any of the above categories as it is a means of implementation. According to the authors, individual SDGs can be a means to achieve other goals, and they suggest implementing all SDGs to achieve sustainable development.

Elder et al. (2016) question the proposed means to achieve all SDGs, because, they claim, some can be used as facilitators to reach others. This interpretation highlights the importance of understanding the interrelationships between all of the goals.

The United Nations Global Sustainable Development Report promotes the social change necessary for sustainable development through institutional and legal arrangements, market mechanisms, and partnerships with public authorities and community associations (United Nations, 2015). The report highlights the urgency of implementing change by proposing the following six entry points related to achieving SDG sub-goals:

• Energy decarbonization with universal access
• Food systems and nutritional models
• Global environmental commons
• Sustainable and just economies
• Urban and peri-urban development
• Well-being and human capabilities

The UN report also identifies the following four levers to implement at each entry point to bring about social change:

• Economy and finance
• Government
• Individual and collective action
• Science and technology

Sustainability and the SDGs are a fundamental part of sustainable development, as they are a means by which companies can acquire and maintain operational legitimacy. Stakeholders are increasingly interested in knowing how companies contribute to the well-being of society, and they measure their performance by evaluating the three perspectives of the TBL approach: economic, social, and environmental.

Consumers' increasing attention regarding the environment and social sustainability resulted in the need to adopt greener business practices and rely on partners who engage in socially responsible behaviors (Caniato et al., 2012; Gazzola et al., 2020). Therefore, companies' sustainable strategies must bring benefits in terms of economic growth, environmental protection, and social equity. Their business activity should generate positive impacts in each of these three areas. Companies should approach sustainability as an opportunity for the future, and managers should provide more value to eco-friendly products without damaging their brand identity (De Angelis et al., 2017). This involves the need for an articulated plan to address sustainability, including policies to create long-term value and innovation to develop scalable and replicable business models (Todeschini et al., 2017). The proposed development model supports a radical change with a systemic vision of sustainability, where the activities of businesses and non-profit organizations must be integrated with political agendas. The agenda indicates how to incorporate public policies into companies, non-profit organizations, and individual behaviors by developing and implementing a long-term vision. Pedersen et al. (2018) supported this idea, showing that companies that adopt innovative business models are more likely to have a proactive sustainability agenda. The SDGs encourage the adoption of sustainable strategies to meet societal expectations (Clarke-Sather & Cobb, 2019). This is especially true for SMEs, such as B Corps, which can become more responsible by undertaking innovative activities (Ferauge, 2012).

The SDGs conform with the Directive 2014/95/EU of the European Parliament and the Council and Legislative Decree No. 254/2016 (Gazzola et al., 2020a). To encourage companies to pursue the SDGs and communicate them in the sustainability report, United Nations Global Compact (UNGC)[4] and the Global Reporting Initiative (GRI) have implemented the project called Reporting on the SDGs (Gazzola et al., 2020a).

In 2020, Gazzola et al. (2020a) analyzed the SDGs' impact on companies' operations and strategies using a sample of 63 Italian public interest companies with data from 2017 to 2020. First, they demonstrated that from 2018 to 2020 the number of clicks required to access non-financial documents in the companies' websites decreased (Gazzola et al., 2020a). Second, they showed that from 2017 to 2020, 35% of companies increased the number of SDGs they pursued, while 6% decreased the number of SDGs they pursued (Gazzola et al., 2020a). The most pursued SDGs were gender equality (5), decent work and economic growth (8), and responsible consumption and production (12) (Gazzola et al., 2020a). The authors affirmed that these SDGs are the most pursued because Italian laws regulate gender equality, sustainable business models, labor, and incentives for economic growth (Gazzola et al., 2020a). Gazzola et al.'s results affirm the findings of Albareda et al. (2006) and Romolini et al. (2014), proving that government policies drive corporate social responsibility in Italian companies.

In the third edition of the *National Observatory on Non-Financial Reporting*, Deloitte confirmed that 115 companies (57% of the total) cited the SDGs in their 2019 NFS. The percentage increased from 44% in 2018 (Amelio et al., 2021). In 2019, the most cited SDGs were decent work and growth (8, 83%), climate action (13, 81%), responsible consumption and production (12, 77%), affordable and clean energy (7, 69%), and industry, innovation and infrastructure (9, 68%) (Amelio et al., 2021). Amelio et al.'s (2021) findings partially agree with Gazzola et al. (2020a) because both identified decent work and economic growth (8) and responsible consumption and production (12) as the most pursued SDGs. In 2019, 60% of the sampled companies included SDGs in specific objectives and targets, which was an increase from 36% in 2018 (Amelio et al., 2021). Thus, the results suggest that companies are increasingly including SDGs in their sustainability strategies.

1.6 The role of stakeholders

The 2030 Agenda emphasizes the participation of all stakeholders in sustainable development. Indeed, to reach the 2030 SDGs, attention to stakeholders is becoming more and more important. We consider economic organizations as more than producers of wealth; they are also social systems, capable of responding to environmental and organizational uncertainties. They can respond to threats and exploit opportunities to survive (Nadler & Tushman, 1990). According to theorists and strategists, any consideration of organizations must include both their internal and external environments. The problem is that environments are subject to changes. Many organizations feel the weight of uncertainty, which tends to oppress visionary leaps and crush the passions and interests of employees (Colombo & Gazzola, 2013).

Most of the time, environmental volatility is unpredictable, and only a good information system can help organizations be prepared (Seilheimer, 2000; Lee et al., 2002). Uncertainty is dangerous because it's difficult to calculate and, therefore, difficult to manage. In a global and rapidly changing environment, an organization can face uncertainty and transform it into opportunity when it can alter its resource base to achieve congruence with the changing environment. This is the dynamic capacity required for contemporary organizations to be successful (Teece, 2014).

In an increasingly interdependent and turbulent globalized world, the isolated advancement of singular interests and partial solutions are not efficient. Achieving the UN's SDGs will require team effort. Organizations are fundamental part of the process, but they cannot accomplish this work alone. All stakeholders must participate in the process to create synergies that will help amplify businesses' positive impact.

1.7 Stakeholder networks and dialogue

A strong interest in stakeholder theory developed in the early 1980s thanks to the theoretical analysis of Freeman and Reed (1983), who proposed the following definition of stakeholder: "any group or individual who can affect or is affected by the achievement of the organization's objectives" (p. 46). In management literature, the term stakeholder was originally defined as those groups without whose support the organization could not survive (Freeman, 1994; Elias & Cavana, 2000). Alkhafaji (1989) also contributed to the understanding of this concept. To explain the dynamics, he defined stakeholders as the groups to whom the corporation is responsible (Elias & Cavana, 2000). Regardless of the specific definition one chooses to apply, stakeholder theory can help managers make decisions by asking them to consider the reciprocal influences that link stakeholders to the organization and vice versa and to identify the effects of those influences (Mella & Gazzola, 2015).

The first concept we analyze is multi-stakeholder dialogue. In recent literature, "stakeholder dialogue" has been identified as a specific and critical capability, leading firms to develop a dynamic capacity for multi-stakeholder interactions. From a social point of view, Zollo and Verona (2011) suggest that the literature on dynamic capabilities should also consider human behavior, including elements such as emotion, motivation, and identity, as components of the change outcomes that will influence various aspects of performance.

From a market-focused sustainability perspective (Hult, 2011), an organization has to consider not only the market-oriented product needs and wants of customers but also the interests of multiple stakeholders concerned with social responsibility issues. However, the critical importance of stakeholder engagement and partnerships was already acknowledged in the basic set-up of the SDGs.

In the context of sustainable development, an organization's stakeholders must evaluate its performance positively in all three of the TBL dimensions: financial, environmental, and social. This may be made possible through inclusive and authentic stakeholder dialogue. Stakeholder dialogue is defined as an organization's ability to interact with stakeholders (Kaptein & van Tulder, 2017). It is essential for organizations to integrate stakeholder insights into their innovation process. Stakeholder dialogue and stakeholder knowledge integration generate innovations according to stakeholder needs. Moreover, stakeholder dialogue uses organizational resources that promote two-way communication, transparency, and appropriate feedback to stakeholders (Ayuso et al., 2006). Organizations do not simply respond to each stakeholder individually. Stakeholders are connected in a network of influences, and organizations must consider the interaction of multiple influences from the different stakeholder groups. Furthermore, an organization is not necessarily at the center of the network but rather a stakeholder in its relevant social system. Freeman and Evan (1990) consider stakeholder relations as "a series of multilateral contracts," as a network of influences. According to them, the organization itself is part of a broader stakeholder environment made of several stakeholders interacting at several levels between themselves and between each of them and the enterprise (Freeman & Evan, 1990).

Stakeholder networks are becoming more and more relevant (Powell, 1990). Hill and Jones (1992) use the agency-stakeholder model to analyze the firm as a nexus of contracts among stakeholders: the authors present the structure of management-stakeholder contracts and the form of the institutional structures that monitor and enforce these contracts between managers and stakeholders. Mitchell et al. (1997) developed a classification of stakeholders, identifying them by the possession or attributed possession of one or more of three relationship attributes: power, legitimacy, and urgency (the last refers to a process whereby stakeholders get importance in managers' minds). De Bakker and den Hond (2008) also consider stakeholders competing to gain salience, operating in a stakeholder network that asks organizations to decide which of them to prioritize over others when managing stakeholder issues.

Multi-stakeholder interactions enable organizations to work together with multiple stakeholders to solve social and environmental issues. Interactions with multiple stakeholders lead to organizations that are better able to respond to environmental pressures. Furthermore, the insights they obtain can drive the development of new markets and create opportunities for growth (Dentoni & Peterson, 2011).

According to Sciarelli and Tani (2013), stakeholder management theory should grant more importance to the stakeholder network. They claim that taking into account stakeholder requests—or failing to do so—can have a far greater effect on an enterprise than what is possible to explain by looking only at the relationship between the enterprise and its direct stakeholders. The stakeholder network approach can help managers identify the role of various stakeholders and determine how they relate to each other. Another benefit of this approach is that it helps managers to see the company's position in the network structure and, thus, to understand the real power or influence they can leverage to achieve the firm's objectives (Rowley, 1997).

Communication, in the form of strategic conversations, with stakeholders is essential in creating shared value for an organization. A friendly relationship with potential clients, NPOs, citizens, governments, and other stakeholders, and a dialogue with them through positive feedback and feed-forwards represent important keys to competitiveness. However, the traditional vision of sustainability fails the challenge by separating stakeholder engagement from business (Colombo & Gazzola, 2013).

Another essential characteristic of stakeholders is their dynamics, which change over time: new stakeholders have to be added, while others may drop out (Elias & Cavana, 2000). The concept of stakeholder dynamics was acknowledged by Freeman (1984 and 2010), and according to him, stakeholders change over time and their stakes change depending on the strategic issue under consideration.

Notes

1 The Post-2015 Development Agenda was a process that began in 2012 and ended in 2015 in which the United Nations defined the future global development framework as a successor to the Millennium Development Goals.

2 The MDGs were eight international development goals that helped to promote political accountability, global awareness, improved metrics, public pressure, and social feedback. They were established in 2000, following the adoption of the UN's Millennium Declaration by the Millennium Summit. These goals were based on the OECD DAC International Development Goals. The eight goals aimed to eliminate poverty and hunger, promote gender equality and empower women, achieve universal primary education, reduce infant mortality, fight HIV/AIDS and malaria, improve maternal health, ensure environmental sustainability, and develop a global partnership for development.

3 The TBL is an accounting framework first developed by John Elkington in 1994. According to Elkington, the bottom line of the profit and loss account (i.e., the net income) does not give a sufficient understanding of a firm's actual value. To better evaluate corporate performance, companies should measure their social, environmental, and financial impact. Unlike other accounting frameworks, it includes the environmental and social dimensions, which are difficult to measure.

4 UNGC is a United Nations initiative to encourage companies to implement universal sustainability principles, support the United Nations goals (SDGs), and publish the results of their actions.

References

Agyeman, J., Bullard, R.D., & Evans, B. (2002). Exploring the nexus: Bringing together sustain- ability, environmental justice and equity. *Space & Polity, 6*(1), 77–90. 10.1080/13562570220137907

Albareda, L., Tencati, A., Lozano, J.M., & Perrini, F. (2006). The government's role in promoting corporate responsibility: A comparative analysis of Italy and UK from the relational state perspective. *Corporate Governance, 6*(4), 386–400. 10.1108/14720700610689504

Alkhafaji, A.F. (1989). *A stakeholder approach to corporate governance: Managing in a dynamic environment.* Praeger.

Amelio, F., Demartini, M.C., Dallai, S., & Mara, F. (2021). Osservatorio Nazionale sulla Rendicontazione Non Finanziaria. *Deloitte*, 1–54.

Andrews, R.N. (1997). National environmental policies: The United States. *National environmental policies: A comparative study of capacity building* (pp. 25–43).

Assembly, U.N.G. (1987). Report of the world commission on environment and development: Our common future. *Development and International Co-operation: Environment.* Oslo, Norway: United Nations General Assembly.

Ayuso, S., Rodriguez, M.A., & Ricart, J.E. (2006). Responsible competitiveness at the "micro"level of the firm: Using stakeholder dialogue as a source for new ideas: A dynamic capability underlying sustainable innovation. *Corporate Governance, 6*(4), 475–490.

Beatley, T., Timothy, B., & Manning, K. (1998). *The ecology of place: Planning for environment, economy, and community.* Washington, DC: Island Press.

Berke, P.R., & Conroy, M.M. (2000). Are we planning for sustainable development? An evaluation of 30 comprehensive plans. *Journal of the American Planning Association, 66*(1), 21–33. 10.1080/01944360008976081

Caniato, F., Caridi, M., Crippa, L., & Moretto, A. (2012). Environmental sustainability in fashion supply chains: An exploratory case-based research.

International Journal of Production Economics, *135*(2), 659–670. 10.1016/j.ijpe.2 011.06.001

Clarke-Sather, A., & Cobb, K. (2019). Onshoring fashion: Worker sustainability impacts of global and local apparel production. *Journal of Cleaner Production*, *208*, 1206–1218. 10.1016/j.jclepro.2018.09.073

Colombo, G., & Gazzola, P. (2013). Aesthetics and ethics of the sustainable organizations. *European Scientific Journal*, *9*(10), 291–301. 10.19044/esj.2013. v9n10p%25p

Dahl, A.L. (1996). *The eco principle: Ecology and economics in symbiosis*. Zed Books.

De Angelis, M., Adıgüzel, F., & Amatulli, C. (2017). The role of design similarity in consumers' evaluation of new green products: An investigation of luxury fashion brands. *Journal of Cleaner Production*, *141*, 1515–1527. 10.1016/ j.jclepro.2016.09.230

de Bakker, F.G., & den Hond, F. (2008). Introducing the politics of stakeholder influence: A review essay. *Business & Society*, *47*(1), 8–20. 10.1177/00076503073 06637

Dentoni, D., & Peterson, H.C. (2011). Multi-stakeholder sustainability alliances in agri-food chains: A framework for multi-disciplinary research. *International Food and Agribusiness Management Review*, *14*(1030-2016-82784), 83–108.

Desa, U.N. (2016). *Transforming our world: The 2030 agenda for sustainable development*. United Nations, 5–40.

Edwards, A.R. (2005). *The sustainability revolution: Portrait of a paradigm shift*. New Society Publishers.

Elder, M., Bengtsson, M., & Akenji, L. (2016). An optimistic analysis of the means of implementation for sustainable development goals: Thinking about goals as means. *Sustainability*, *8*(9), 962. 10.3390/su8090962

Elias, A.A., & Cavana, R.Y. (2000, December). Stakeholder analysis for systems thinking and modeling. In *Victoria University of Wellington, New Zealand. Conference paper.*

Emas, R. (2015). The concept of sustainable development: Definition and defining principles. *Brief for GSDR*, *2015*, 10–13140. 10.13140/RG.2.2.34980.22404

Ferauge, P. (2012). A conceptual framework of corporate social responsibility and innovation. *Global Journal of Business Research*, *6*(5), 85–96. https://ssrn. com/abstract=2146107

Ferioli, M. (2022). B Corp: Un Nuovo Modello di Business per la Mobilità Sostenibile. Il Caso del Gruppo Maganetti. *Economia Aziendale Online*, *13*(1), 53–73. 10.13132/2038-5498/13.1.53-73

Freeman, R.E. (1984 and 2010). *Strategic management: A stakeholder approach*. Cambridge University Press.

Freeman, R.E. (1994). The politics of stakeholder theory: Some future directions. *Business Ethics Quarterly*, 409–421. 10.2307/3857340

Freeman, R.E., & Evan, W.M. (1990). Corporate governance: A stakeholder interpretation. *Journal of Behavioral Economics*, *19*(4), 337–359. 10.1016/ 0090-5720(90)90022-Y

Freeman, R.E., & Reed, D.L. (1983). Stockholders and stakeholders: A new perspective on corporate governance. *California Management Review*, *25*(3), 88–106. 10.2307/41165018

Gazzola, P., Pavione, E., & Dall'Ava, M. (2020). I differenti significati di sostenibilità per le aziende del lusso e della moda: Case studies a confronto. *Economia Aziendale Online*, *10*(4), 663–676. 10.13132/2038-5498/10.4.2005

Gazzola, P., Pezzetti, R., Amelio, S., & Grechi, D. (2020a). Non-financial information disclosure in Italian public interest companies: A sustainability reporting perspective. *Sustainability*, *12*(15), 6063. 10.3390/su12156063

Gow, D.D. (1992). Poverty and natural resources: Principles for environmental management and sustainable development. *Environmental Impact Assessment Review*, *12*(1–2), 49–65. 10.1016/0195-9255(92)90005-I

Hatfield Dodds, S. (2000). Pathways and paradigms for sustaining human communities. In *Sustaining Human Settlements: A Challenge for the New Millennium*. The Urban International Press, North Shields, 30–43.

Haughton, G. (1999). Environmental justice and the sustainable city. *Journal of Planning Education and Research*, *18*(3), 233–243. 10.1177/0739456X9901800305

Hill, C.W., & Jones, T.M. (1992). Stakeholder-agency theory. *Journal of Management Studies*, *29*(2), 131–154. 10.1111/j.1467-6486.1992.tb00657.x

Hult, G.T.M. (2011). Market-focused sustainability: Market orientation plus!. *Journal of the Academy of Marketing Science*, *39*(1), 1–6. 10.1007/s11747-010-0223-4

Italia, G. (2019). Inquinamento atmosferico e cambiamenti climatici - Elementi per una strategia nazionale di prevenzione. *In Workshop*, *26*, 7–11.

Jabareen, Y. (2004). A knowledge map for describing variegated and conflict domains of sustainable development. *Journal of Environmental Planning and Management*, *47*(4), 623–642. 10.1080/0964056042000243267

Jabareen, Y. (2008). A new conceptual framework for sustainable development. *Environment, Development and Sustainability*, *10*(2), 179–192. 10.1007/s10668-006-9058-z

Kaptein, M., & Van Tulder, R. (2017). Toward effective stakeholder dialogue. *Business and Society Review*, *108*(2), 203–224. 10.1111/1467-8594.00161

Lawrence, R.J. (2020). Overcoming barriers to implementing sustainable development goals. *Human Ecology Review*, *26*(1), 95–116. https://www.jstor.org/stable/27027239

Lee, S., Koh, S., Yen, D., & Tang, H.L. (2002). Perception gaps between IS academics and IS practitioners: An exploratory study. *Information & Management*, *40*(1), 51–61. 10.1016/S0378-7206(01)00132-X

Mashado des Johansson, N., & Burns, T.R. (2012). Not bystanders any longer: Social sciences, social responsibility and sustainability research in an emerging revolution. In *Proceedings of the CRIARS Conference*, Lisbon 25–27 October 2012.

Mella, P., & Gazzola, P. (2015). Ethics builds reputation. *International Journal of Markets and Business Systems*, *1*(1), 38–52.

Mitchell, R.K., Agle, B.R., & Wood, D.J. (1997). Toward a theory of stakeholder identification and salience: Defining the principle of who and what really counts. *Academy of Management Review*, *22*(4), 853–886. 10.5465/amr.1997.9711022105

Morton, S., Pencheon, D., & Squires, N. (2017). Sustainable Development Goals (SDGs), and their implementation: A national global framework for health, development and equity needs a systems approach at every level. *British Medical Bulletin*, 1–10. 10.1093/bmb/ldx031

Nadler, D.A., & Tushman, M.L. (1990). Beyond the charismatic leader: Leadership and organizational change. *California Management Review, 32*(2), 77–97. 10.1016/S0268-4012(00)00017-7

Pearce, D., Barbier, E., & Markandya, A. (2013). *Sustainable development: Economics and environment in the Third World*. Routledge.

Pearce, D.W., & Turner, R.K. (1989). *Economics of natural resources and the environment*. Johns Hopkins University Press.

Pedersen, E.R.G., Gwozdz, W., & Hvass, K.K. (2018). Exploring the relationship between business model innovation, corporate sustainability, and organisational values within the fashion industry. *Journal of Business Ethics, 149*(2), 267–284. 10.1007/s10551-016-3044-7

Powell, W.W. (1990). Neither market nor hierarchy. In *Sociology of organizations: Structures and relationships* (pp. 30–40). Sage publications.

Redclift, M. (1993). *Sustainable development: Concepts, contradictions, and conflicts. Food for the future: Conditions and contradictions of sustainability*. John Wiley.

Redclift, M., & Sage, C. (1994). *Strategies for sustainable development: Local agendas for the Southern Hemisphere*. Chichester (United Kingdom) Wiley.

Redclift, M.R. (1987). *Sustainable development: Exploring the contradictions*. John Wiley and Sons.

Romolini, A., Fissi, S., & Gori, E. (2014). Scoring CSR reporting in listed companies—evidence from Italian best practices. *Corporate Social Responsibility and Environmental Management, 21*(2), 65–81. 10.1002/csr.1299

Rowley, T.J. (1997). Moving beyond dyadic ties: A network theory of stakeholder influences. *Academy of Management Review, 22*(4), 887–910. 10.5465/amr.1 997.9711022107

Sachs, J.D. (2012). From millennium development goals to sustainable development goals. *The Lancet, 379*(9832), 2206–2211. 10.1016/S0140-6736(12)60685-0

Sachs, W. (1999). *Planet dialectics: Essays on ecology, equity, and the end of development*. Zed Books.

Scherer, A.G., & Palazzo, G. (2008). Globalization and corporate social responsibility. In A. Crane, A. McWilliams, D. Matten, J. Moon, & D. Siegel (Eds.), *The Oxford handbook of corporate social responsibility* (pp. 413–431). Oxford University Press.

Sciarelli, M., & Tani, M. (2013). Network approach and stakeholder management. *Business Systems Review, 2*, 175–190. 10.7350/BSR.V09.2013

Seilheimer, S.D. (2000). Information management during systems development: A model for improvement in productivity. *International Journal of Information Management, 20*(4), 287–295.

Solow, R. (1992). *An almost practical step toward sustainability; an invited lecture on the occasion of the Fortieth Anniversary of Resources for the Future* (No. AV 333.716 no. 13). Resources for the Future, Washington, DC (EUA).

Teece, D.J. (2014). A dynamic capabilities-based entrepreneurial theory of the multinational enterprise. *Journal of International Business Studies, 45*(1), 8–37. 10.1057/jibs.2013.54

Todeschini, B.V., Cortimiglia, M N., Callegaro-de-Menezes, D., & Ghezzi, A. (2017). Innovative and sustainable business models in the fashion industry: Entrepreneurial drivers, opportunities, and challenges. *Business Horizons, 60*(6), 759–770. 10.1016/j.bushor.2017.07.003

United Nations. (2002). *Report of the World Summit on Sustainable Development*. United Nations. digitallibrary.un.org/record/478154?ln=en

United Nations. (2015). *Transforming our world: The 2030 agenda for sustainable development*. United Nations. digitallibrary.un.org/record/478154?ln=en

Werna, E., & Lawrence, R. (2009). *Labour conditions for construction: Building cities, decent work and the role of local authorities*. John Wiley & Sons.

World Commission on Environment and Development. (1987). *Our common future* [The Brundtland Report]. Oxford University Press.

Zollo, M., & Verona, G. (2011). Understanding the human side of dynamic capabilities: Towards a holistic model. In *Handbook of Organizational Learning and Knowledge Management* (vol. 2, pp. 535–550). Oxford University Press.

2 Corporate social responsibility
The new imperative

2.1 Corporate social responsibility definitions

The literature on Corporate social responsibility (CSR) is extensive, and the interest in this topic is increasing in research and in practice (Meuer et al., 2020). Events such as recent financial and stock market failures, slow economic development, and environmental scandals led to the evolution of this concept (Gazzola, 2012c). Since its birth, many authors and institutions have defined it. Therefore, it has different interpretations depending on the culture in which it is applied (Carroll, 1999; Mazurkiewicz, 2004; Romolini et al., 2014; Feng & Ngai, 2020). For this reason, there is a lack of clarity between practitioners and researchers, making it difficult to distinguish among sustainable practices. This means that, potentially, every company's activity can be labeled as sustainable even if it is not, thus generating the greenwashing phenomenon (Meuer et al., 2020). Therefore, most governments have introduced standards in their legal codes (Mazurkiewicz, 2004). The lack of a single definition was recognized as early as 1999 by Carroll in his article "Corporate Social Responsibility: Evolution of a Definitional Construct" (Carroll, 1999; Nave & Ferreira, 2019). The more recent and the most-cited definitions are as follows:

- Carroll, in 1979, declared that "the social responsibility of business encompasses the economic, legal, ethical, and discretionary expectations that society has of organizations at a given point in time" (p. 500). The author wanted to highlight that economic and social concerns are linked.
- The World Business Council for Sustainable Development defined CSR as "the continuing commitment by business to behave ethically and contribute to economic development while improving the quality of life of the workforce and their families as well as of the local community and society at large" (WBCSD, 1998) This definition considers the environmental dimension of CSR (Gazzola, 2012c).

DOI: 10.4324/9781003388470-3

- The European Union (EU) defined CSR as "a concept whereby companies integrate social and environmental concerns in their business operations and in their interaction with their stakeholders on a voluntary basis" (Commission of the European Communities, 2001, p. 8). This implies that companies should voluntarily plan both economic and social objectives. Therefore, companies are considered socially responsible if they make human capital and environmental investments, maintain positive relationships with stakeholders, and consider their legal expectations. In 2011, the EU definition was simplified as follows: "the responsibility of enterprises for their impacts on society" (European Commission, 2011, p. 6). The new definition expands the concept of sustainability by including all the impacts on society. Thus, sustainable companies must collaborate with all stakeholders by integrating ethical, social, environmental, human rights, and consumer concerns into their business strategies (European Commission, 2011). Companies' objectives must maximize the shared value for their shareholders and society and must identify and avoid possible negative impacts (European Commission, 2011).
- According to the Business for Social Responsibility's definition, CSR means running a business "to meet or exceed the ethical, legal, commercial and public expectations that the company has towards business. CSR is seen by leadership companies as more than a collection of discrete practices or occasional gestures or initiatives motivated by marketing, public relations, or other business benefits. Rather, it is viewed as a comprehensive set of policies, practices, and programs that are integrated throughout business operations, and decision-making processes that are supported and rewarded by top management" (Mazurkiewicz, 2004, p. 4).
- The World Bank defined CSR as "the commitment of business to contribute to sustainable economic development—working with employees, their families, the local community and society at large to improve the quality of life, in ways that are both good for business and good for development" (Ward, 2004, p. 3).

All these definitions focus on the companies' actions and highlight the need to operate in a way that preserves society and the environment. Therefore, it is clear that the concept of CSR involves the need to undertake sustainable activities that incorporate social and environmental aspects into companies' economic and financial activities (Gazzola, 2012c). In this way, CSR activities and practices represent both a financial investment and a competitive strategy that includes social, ethical, and environmental concerns. This allows companies to improve their resources and processes (Arru & Ruggieri, 2016). The concept of CSR aligns with the three pillars that make up the triple bottom line

(TBL) approach (Crane & Matten, 2021): economic prosperity, environmental quality, and social justice (Gazzola, 2012a; Gazzola & Mella, 2012). In this way, CSR encompasses the following five dimensions (Dahlsrud, 2008; Nave & Ferreira, 2019):

1 *Social*: The relationship between business and society
2 *Environmental*: Responsibility for the environment
3 *Stakeholders*: Responsibility toward the different stakeholders
4 *Economic*: Socioeconomic aspects, financial aspects, and those related to the companies' operations
5 *Voluntariness*: All the actions not required by law

CSR requires companies to produce shared value for the business and society because they are considered social-economic actors (Gazzola & Mella, 2012).

2.2 The historical evolution of CSR

2.2.1 The birth of CSR

The birth of the CSR concept can be traced back to the Industrial Revolution (1760–1840) when the increasing number of large companies made it possible to recognize that corporations have some responsibilities toward the labor force and their employees (Evans et al., 2013). An example was set by Robert Owen, who recognized the need for his company to improve their policies regarding employees' well-being by ensuring that they had access to decent working conditions, decent housing, and education for their children (Evans et al., 2013). However, few companies followed his example (Evans et al., 2013).

In the 1910s, Frederick Winslow Taylor recognized a mutual interest and equality of responsibility between workers and companies; therefore, he argued that they should collaborate (Evans et al., 2013). This declaration was followed by Henry Gantt's claim that businesses must behave responsibly toward society, otherwise the community will take over (Evans et al., 2013).

In the 1920s, the CSR concept was further influenced by the emergence of large modern corporations and society's rapidly transforming characteristics (Hoffman, 2007). In those years, the idea that maintaining industrial harmony required social ethics to replace individual ethics spread in American society (Hoffman, 2007). Thus, executives of large public companies began to see social responsibility as a tool to legitimize their positions in society (Hoffman, 2007). Robert Hay and Ed Gray defined the post-1920s period as the "trusteeship management phase" because executives began to be seen as trustees of stakeholders (Carroll, 2008). In fact, managers began to maintain a fair balance between demands coming from different parties (such as employees, customers, and the community) and the need to maximize shareholders' wealth due to the growing diffusion of share ownership and an increasingly pluralistic society (Carroll, 2008). In those years, Henry Ford realized that companies do not operate in isolation from society, solidifying the importance of CSR (Lee, 2008; Evans et al., 2013). In this way, Ford supported the idea that providing services to the society in which one operates overrides the need to generate profits (Lee, 2008; Evans et al., 2013).

2.2.2 The 1930s, 1940s, and 1950s: First publications and the beginning of modern literature

The first publications relating to the topic of CSR date back to the 1930s (Carroll, 1999). The most relevant publications from those years are *The Functions of the Executive* by Chester Barnard, published in 1938, and *Social Control of Business* by J.M. Clark, published in 1939 (Carroll, 1999).

As the concept of trusteeship became widespread among business leaders in the 1940s, companies began to recognize themselves as socially responsible entities simply by becoming anti-communist institutions (Carroll, 2008). In *Measurement of the Social Performance of Business*, Theodore Kreps recognized that the Great Depression increased concerns about corporate social benefits (Kreps, 1962; Carroll, 1999). In this way, he identified social responsibility as a fundamental part of companies' social performance. In the period leading up to the 1950s, companies began to donate as a way to give back to society; thus, Patrick Murphy defined this as the Philanthropic Era (Carroll, 2008).

The 1950s marked the beginning of the Awareness Era (Carroll, 2008). During that period, businesses' responsibility for their community became more widely recognized than it had been in previous years; however, businesswomen were not yet recognized in the literature (Carroll, 2008). The beginning of the modern period of literature and the spread of the concept of CSR was made possible, thanks to the 1953 publication *Social Responsibilities of the Businessman* by Howard Rothmann Bowen (Carroll, 2008; Lee, 2008; Evans et al., 2013; Agudelo et al., 2019). Bowen recognized that, in conducting their business, companies must consider all stakeholders in society (Lee, 2008; Evans et al., 2013). Furthermore, he declared CSR to have positive value and called for it to be encouraged and supported to achieve sustainable development, even if it cannot solve all of society's problems (Lee, 2008). Bowen illustrated what organizational and managerial changes companies could make to address social concerns. Among these were the social education activities of business leaders, the introduction of an ethical code of conduct, changes in the composition of their boards of directors, greater social representation in management, the introduction of social auditing, and greater social science research (Carroll, 2008). Although the issue of CSR was widely discussed in the 1950s, there is no evidence that the social practices and organizational changes recommended by Bowen were actually applied by companies (Carroll, 2008). When the Californian school of the 1950s introduced the concept of CSR, it was understood as the set of business activities aimed at pursuing both a financial advantage for the capitalists and a benefit, even indirect, for society (Gazzola, 2012c). The entrepreneur was expected take on social responsibility; therefore, his actions had to be aligned with the values and objectives of the company (Gazzola, 2012c). In this way, the focus was not on the actions and externalities generated by the companies but on the work done by the managers. In 1957, in *Leadership in Administration*, Selznick stated that organizations must necessarily adapt to society's external forces because these limit organizational flexibility, implying that managers must consider external pressures without allowing any single point of view to dominate decisions affecting the company as a whole (Selznick, 1957; Evans et al., 2013).

2.2.3 The 1960s: Businesses begin to recognize their duties toward society

Starting in the 1960s, social concerns took on increasing relevance, and managers began to meet both shareholder and company expectations (Gazzola, 2012c). Murphy defined the period between 1968 and 1973 as the Issue Era because companies began to focus on specific environmental concerns (Carroll, 2008). According to Carroll (2008), Keith Davis was the most relevant author in those years, and he defined CSR as: "businessmen's decisions and actions taken for reasons at least partially beyond the firm's direct economic or technical interest" (Davis, 1960, p. 70). Davis became famous, thanks to the iron law of responsibility, which stated that "social responsibilities of businessmen need to be commensurate with their social power" (Davis, 1960, p. 71; Carroll, 1999). The author argued that there is a link between power and social responsibility and that these two elements coexist; consequently, he claimed, companies' activities must be undertaken following a socially responsible perspective (Davis, 1960). In their 1966 textbook *Business and Its Environment*, Davis and Robert L. Bloomstorm identified a link between social systems and commercial activity (Carroll, 1999). According to the authors, the concept of CSR requires consideration of the effects of management decisions on the entire social system (Carroll, 1999). The following year, Davis expanded that definition of CSR to include all institutional actions and the resulting impact on the entire social system (Carroll, 1999). Several definitions were subsequently published. In the 1967 book *Corporate Social Responsibility*, Clarence C. Walton recognized that although socially responsible actions were voluntary, economic returns could not be measured directly (Carroll, 1999).

2.2.4 The 1970s: Stakeholder and shareholder theory

The so-called Responsiveness Era began in 1974 (Carroll, 2008). During this period, neoclassical theory and stakeholder theory began to develop, and companies began to take organizational and managerial actions to address social responsibility concerns (Carroll, 2008). Neoclassical theory and stakeholder theory provide conflicting characterizations of the evolution of the concept of CSR. However, as discussed next, they share a fundamental commonality. Neoclassical theory considers efficiency as an unnecessary cost because companies' only concern is profit maximization (Gazzola, 2012c). In "The Social Responsibility of Business Is to Increase Its Profits," the most prominent proponent of this theory, Milton Friedman, argued that social concerns were borne by the state; therefore, companies did not have the responsibility to improve social well-being (Friedman, 1970). Furthermore, the author argued that companies and managers only had to meet the expectations of shareholders; thus, the achievement of socially responsible goals was considered an illegitimate activity carried out at the expense of other shareholders' profits. Friedman had already expressed this theory eight years earlier in his book *Capitalism and Freedom* (1962) in which he argued that "there is one and only one social responsibility of business—to use its resources and engage in activities designed to increase its profits so long as it stays within the rules of the game, which is to say, engages in open and free competition without deception fraud" (Friedman, 1962, p. 133). In contrast, the stakeholder theory argues that ethical and social impacts represent an opportunity to create value for both a company and the environment that it inhabits (Gazzola, 2012c). Proponents of this theory argue that there is a relationship of reciprocal influence between companies and their stakeholders (Gazzola, 2012b, 2012c). Therefore, they claim, companies must envisage specific management objectives and strategies for each category of homogeneous shareholders, identifying those that most influence the company and those capable of mobilizing other stakeholders (Gazzola, 2012c). Although the theories of shareholders and stakeholders conflict, they have one point in common: they agree that the purpose of managers' actions is long-term profitability. Thanks to numerous publications by many exponents of scientific and economic fields, these two theories evolved over the years. In his 1971 book *Business in Contemporary Society: Framework and Issues*, Harold Johnson introduced the first concepts related to stakeholders theory, recognizing that managers had the task of balancing the interests of many social partners (Carroll, 2008). The same year, the Committee for Economic Development (CED) introduced the notion of three concentric circles of social responsibility in the book *Social Responsibilities of Business Corporations*. The CED recognized that businesses had broader social duties than ever (Carroll, 2008). According to this model, it is possible to divide CSR into three groups of responsibilities (Carroll, 2008). The outer circle groups all of the responsibilities that cannot be clearly defined and those associated with social and environmental development (Carroll, 2008). The central circle encloses the social values and priorities—that is, those relating to the conservation of the environment and consumer expectations (Carroll, 2008). Finally, the innermost circle encompasses all basic economic responsibilities and those relating to the economic functions of companies (Carroll, 2008).

In his 1971 book *Business and Society*, George Steiner outlined several methods and models for determining the circumstances in which CSR should be applied (Carroll, 2008). Beginning in 1975, many authors began to focus on distinguishing between the concepts of CSR, corporate social performance (CSP), and corporate social responsiveness. In his article "From CSR_1 to CSR_2: The Maturing of Business and Society Thought," William Frederick clarified that corporate social responsiveness (CSR_2) refers to a corporations' ability to face social pressures and fulfill the community's needs by establishing dedicated procedures, mechanisms, and behavior models (Frederick, 1994). In other words, CSR_2 represents an evolution of the concept of CSR because, for the first-time, concrete ways were provided to reflect the concept of CSR in practice. Carroll (2008) recognized S. Prakash Sethi as one of the greatest writers of the 1970s (Carroll, 2008). Sethi published many articles focused on differentiating between the concepts of CSR, corporate social responsiveness, and CSP (Carroll, 2008). In the 1975 article "Dimensions of Corporate Social Performance: An Analytical Framework," Sethi distinguished between social responsibility, social responsiveness, and social obligations (Sethi, 1975; Carroll, 2008). According to the author, the term "social obligation" is linked to companies' legal and economic responsibilities, while "social responsibility" is related to social values, norms, and performance expectations (Sethi, 1975; Carroll, 2008). Finally, "social responsiveness" concerns the need to meet the community's social needs (Sethi, 1975; Carroll, 2008). In the same year, Lee Preston and James Post contributed to the study of the effect of corporate responsibility on public policies (Carroll, 2008). In 1978, Sandra Holmes recognized that community affairs, charities, pollution control, recruitment, minorities' development, and education support were the leading social problems companies should address when undertaking socially responsible activities (Carroll, 2008). In 1979, Archie B. Carroll defined the concept of CSR as based on "the economic, legal, ethical, and discretionary expectations that society has of organizations" (p. 500). According to Carroll (1979), to increase the social quality of life, companies had to generate benefits for the community, even without an explicit request being made (Carroll, 1979). Therefore, companies had to comply with laws and generate economic value without ignoring social ethics and values (Carroll, 1979).

2.2.5 The 1980s: The evolution of CSR

In the 1980s, the first theories and models were developed to investigate how socially responsible policies can be adopted and how companies' social performance can be measured (Carroll, 2008; Gazzola, 2012c). According to Thomas M. Jones, it was challenging to reach consensus about what constituted a socially responsible behavior at that time. Jones considered CSR to be a process and suggested that companies do have some obligations toward different social groups that go beyond what is prescribed by law or trade union contract (Jones, 1980). Furthermore, during this time, companies voluntarily committed to socially responsible activities, even though their behaviors were influenced by union agreements or laws (Carroll, 2008). In 1981, Frank Tuzzolino and Barry Armandi developed a need-hierarchy framework to evaluate companies' socially responsible behaviors (Carroll, 2008). The framework was based on Maslow's pyramid and Carroll's 1979 definition of CSR (Carroll, 2008). In the authors' view, companies, like people, have some needs (physiological, security, affiliation, esteem, and self-fulfillment) (Carroll, 2008). In *The Evolution of the Corporate Social Performance Model* (1985), Steven Wartick and Philip Cochran extended the integration of social responsibility, responsiveness, and social issues (Carroll, 2008). They reformulated these three concepts into a framework of principles, processes, and policies, arguing that Carroll's (1979) definition had to be interpreted as a set of principles, social responsiveness as a process, and social issues management as policies (Carroll, 2008). In 1987, Edwin M. Epstein defined the corporate social policy process by integrating social responsibility, social responsiveness, and business ethics concepts (Carroll, 2008). Furthermore, Epstein developed a 1980s social responsibility agenda by identifying "business practices and the impact on environmental pollution, urban life and questionable/abusive practices of multinationals" (Carroll, 2008, p. 21) as the most significant topics in those years. In *Stockholders and Stakeholders: A New Perspective on Corporate Governance* (1983), R. Edward Freeman and David L. Reed postulated two definitions of stakeholders, one in a narrower sense and another in a broader sense. According to the latter, stakeholders were "any identifiable group or individual who can affect the achievement of an organization's objectives" (Freeman & Reed, 1983, p. 91). In contrast, according to the narrower sense, they were "any identifiable group or individual on which the organization is dependent for its continued survival" (Freeman & Reed, 1983, p. 91). The two definitions broadened the concept of stakeholders by stressing their importance in influencing companies' activities. Specifically, the broad-sense definition highlighted stakeholders' ability to affect companies' activities, while the narrow-sense definition stressed the legitimacy of the interests they hold. In 1984, Freeman's book on stakeholder theory, *Strategic Management: A Stakeholder Approach*, had a massive impact on the conceptualization of CSR because, after many ethical scandals, public interest shifted to management and the illegal practices of companies (Carroll, 2008). In Freeman's view, managers had to manage the company by ensuring stakeholders' rights and well-being. Furthermore, he recognized that management's goal is long-term corporate survival; thus, managers should act as agents for the company they represent by establishing relationships of trust with their stakeholders (Carroll, 2008). Freeman argued that this would be possible by having stakeholders' representatives participate on the board of directors so that they could influence and closely monitor company activities (Carroll, 2008).

2.2.6 The 1990s: The phenomenon of globalization and the desire for a sustainable future

The globalization process that began in the 1990s increased the visibility of companies, as well as the social expectations placed on them, both in their host countries and their countries of origin, generating greater reputational risk for unsustainable companies (Agudelo et al., 2019). Thus, philanthropic donations became commonplace, and the number of businesses undertaking socially responsible activities, such as strategic giving and cause-related marketing, increased (Carroll, 2008). During those years, international events, such as the foundation of the Business for Social Responsibility (BSR) association, the creation of the European Environment Agency (EEA), the Rio Declaration on Environment and Development, the adoption of the Framework Convention on Climate Change, and the United Nations' Agenda 21 induced the growth of the CSR concept and represented an international effort to improve companies' social responsibility by setting a higher standard for global climate issues (Agudelo et al., 2019). Originally, sustainability was considered strictly in relation to responsibility for the natural environment, while the concepts CSP, business ethics, and corporate citizenship continued to grow (Carroll, 2008). In *The Pyramid of Corporate Social Responsibility* (1991), Carroll prioritized each category of responsibility reported in his 1979 CSR definition.

In the pyramid, the author illustrated the following four leading responsibilities for companies (Carroll, 1991; Agudelo et al., 2019):

1 *Economic responsibilities*: Those fundamental obligations that create a foundation for all the other types of responsibilities
2 *Legal responsibilities*: Those related to not breaching governmental laws and expectations
3 *Ethical responsibilities*: Those aimed at integrating ethic principles and sensitivity into a company's decision-making processes
4 *Philanthropic responsibilities*: Those aligned with the corporate citizenship concept, according to which companies must contribute to improving their community and society's quality of life

In 1994, John Elkington introduced the TBL concept (Agudelo et al., 2019), which is based on three principles: economic prosperity, environmental quality, and social justice (Gazzola, 2012a). According to Elkington, companies must combine social and environmental concerns in their economic and financial activities (Gazzola, 2012a). Starting in 1995, the European Commission (EC) played an important role in fostering the adoption of socially responsible practices and fighting unemployment and social exclusion. Their work led to the adoption of the European Business Declaration against Social Exclusion by 20 companies and the birth of the European Business Network for Social Cohesion (renamed CSR Europe) in 1996 (Agudelo et al., 2019). The same year, in *How Corporate Social Responsibility Pays Off*, Lee Burke and Jeanne M. Logsdon acknowledged, for the first time, that socially responsible activities and behaviors led to financial benefits (Burke & Logsdon, 1996; Agudelo et al., 2019). Furthermore, they identified the following five socially responsible strategic dimensions to efficiently achieve business objectives and create economic value (Burke & Logsdon, 1996; Agudelo et al., 2019):

1 *Centrality*: How much the business's mission and objectives align with their socially responsible activities
2 *Proactivity*: The ability to create policies in anticipation of social trends
3 *Specificity*: The ability to generate private benefits
4 *Visibility*: The relevance of the observable and recognizable socially responsible activities to stakeholders
5 *Voluntarism*: The discretionary decision-making process not influenced by external compliance requirements

In 1997, Ronald K. Mitchell, Bradley R. Agle, and Donna J. Wood identified three classes of stakeholders based on their power, urgency, and legitimacy (Mitchell et al., 1997). This theory represents a positive contribution to the development of stakeholder theory.

Laten stakeholders, which are those with limited resources, time, and energy, comprise the first class. They have little power to influence management's work because they have only one requirement (Mitchell et al., 1997). This class includes the following three stakeholder types:

1 *Dormant*: Those with the power to impose their will on a company with little or no interaction with the firm and with no urgent claims or legitimate relationships
2 *Discretionary*: Those who have legitimacy but cannot influence the company and have no urgent claims
3 *Demanding*: Those with urgent claims but neither power nor legitimacy (Mitchell et al., 1997)

The second class is composed of expectant stakeholders, who have more justified claims and are more relevant to management, as they fit two of the three requirements (Mitchell et al., 1997). This class includes the following three stakeholder types:

1 *Dominant*: Those who have the power and legitimacy to take management attention
2 *Dependent*: Those who depend on the firm because they have legitimacy and urgency
3 *Dangerous*: Those who represent a danger for the company because they have power and urgency (Mitchell et al., 1997)

Finally, the last class of stakeholders possesses all three requirements; thus, they have priority and the company's attention (Mitchell et al., 1997).

2.2.7 The 2000s: CSR as a strategic development tool

In the 2000s, the research on CSR focused on companies' interactions with the external environment. Using an empirical approach, many publications proved that CSP and CSR were related to other important variables (Carroll, 2008). For example, Bryan Husted discussed how CSP derives "from the nature of the social issue and its corresponding strategies and structures" (Husted, 2000, p. 24). He considered stakeholder management, issues management, and corporate social responsiveness as a single concept (Carroll, 2008). In March 2000, thanks to the Lisbon European Council, CSR entered the European Union Agenda and became a strategic tool for creating a socially cohesive and more competitive society to strengthen and modernize the European social model. In 2001, the "Green Paper" of the Commission of European Communities defined CSR as "a concept whereby companies integrate social and environmental concerns in their business operations and in their interaction with their stakeholders on a voluntary basis" (Commission of the European Communities, 2001, p. 8). The Commission of European Communities (2001) clarified that socially responsible companies had to invest in the environment, human capital, and relations with their stakeholders while also meeting legal expectations. Therefore, business policies and strategies had to embrace social, environmental, and economic goals (Commission of the European Communities, 2001). The same year, in "Changes in Corporate Practices in Response to Public Interest Advocacy and Actions," N. Craig Smith defined CSR as

> the obligations of the firm to its stakeholders—people affected by corporate policies and practices. These obligations go beyond legal requirements and the firm's duties to its shareholders. Fulfillment of these obligations is intended to minimize any harm and maximize the long-run beneficial impact of the firm on society. (Smith, 2001, p. 142)

Smith wanted to stress that in order to create long-term benefits for society companies must incorporate socially responsible activities into their strategies. Following this idea, the same year, Lantos introduced the strategic CSR concept, claiming that social responsibility is a strategic variable when it is part of management's strategies (Lantos, 2001; Agudelo et al., 2019). The author declared that companies would only adopt socially responsible practices if doing so would bring financial returns. Thus, he placed the economic variable at the basis of socially responsible behavior (Agudelo et al., 2019). In 2002, Kristin Backhaus, Brett A. Stone, and Karl Heiner investigated the relationship between employer attractiveness and CSP, revealing that when people are choosing a job, they consider CSP to be a positive variable (Carroll, 2008). Furthermore, they revealed that job seekers mainly evaluate companies using five drivers: environment, employee relations, diversity, community relations, and product issues (Carroll, 2008). This conclusion represented a breakthrough in the literature, as people's concern for a sustainable and healthy workplace was recognized for the first time (Carroll, 2008). In *Stakeholder Theory and Organizational Ethics* (2003), Robert Phillips combined stakeholder theory and the moral and political theory of John Rawls to develop an organizational ethics theory. He declared that organizational ethics, as distinct from ethics applied to human activities, was needed inside companies (Phillips, 2003). Furthermore, the author acknowledged the presence of moral obligations within organizations and among stakeholders, thus supporting the principle of proportionality and stakeholders' fairness (Phillips, 2003). The first principle binds obligations to benefits, while the second one binds companies and stakeholders to moral obligations (Phillips, 2003). Phillips classified stakeholders as follows:

- *Normative*: Those with priority, as they own a normative bond with the company
- *Derivative*: Those who claim a "moral conscience" and own moral legitimacy

In his book, Phillips admitted some ambiguities about the priority of stakeholder categories, first declaring that managers should not consider social activists as normative stakeholders, but later affirming that civil disobedience in the name of community values makes activists normative stakeholders (Phillips, 2003). In the same year, M.S. Schwartz and Archie B. Carroll developed a three-domain approach to CSR (Carroll, 2008). The authors revealed that philanthropy could be interpreted in both ethical and discretionary terms and showed the organizational characteristics helpful for firms' analysis (Carroll, 2008). In 2003, Marcel van Marrewijk criticized the definitions of CSR, corporate citizenship, sustainable development, sustainable entrepreneurship, TBL, and business ethics. He distinguished corporate sustainability and CSR according to companies' development stages, awareness, and ambition levels (Van Marrewijk, 2003). In *Corporate Social Responsibility: Doing the Best for Your Company and Your Cause* (2005), Philip Kotler and Nancy Lee identified 25 socially responsible business practices and investments to support companies. The authors' aim was to "guide the decision making of corporate managers, executives, and their staff besieged on a daily basis with requests and proposals for the support of social causes" (Kotler & Lee, 2005, p. 1). They classified business practices into the following six social initiatives (Kotler & Lee, 2005; Perrini, 2006; Carroll, 2008):

1 *Cause promotion*: Increasing consideration and awareness of social issues
2 *Cause-related marketing*: Contributing to causes according to increases in the level of sales
3 *Community volunteering*: Employees contributing to the community with their time and talents
4 *Corporate philanthropy*: Direct contribution to causes
5 *Corporate social marketing*: Behavior change initiatives
6 *Socially responsible business practices*: Discretionary investments and activities to support the alleviation of social problems

The authors recommended that companies to prioritize the social initiatives that bring the highest benefit to them and society (Kotler & Lee, 2005; Perrini, 2006). Furthermore, they defined CSR as "a commitment to improving community well-being through discretionary business practices and contributions of corporate resources" (Kotler & Lee, 2005, p. 3; Perrini, 2006, p. 91). Kotler and Lee saw the CSR concept in a broad sense. Thus, socially responsible actions must not be undertaken only as a philanthropic initiative or a mere marketing tool, but to improve society's well-being (Kotler& Lee, 2005; Perrini, 2006). Their idea was followed by Michael E. Porter and Mark R. Kramer (2006), who declared that if socially responsible activities are envisioned only as a marketing tool to improve a company's image or to achieve the legitimacy to operate, the potential social benefits will be counter-productive and limited (Porter & Kramer, 2006).

2.2.8 The 2010s: Shared value theory and the global expansion of CSR

In 2011, the European Union definition was simplified to: "the respon-sibility of enterprises for their impacts on society" (European Commission, 2011, p. 6). The new definition encompasses all of a company's impacts on society, including the environment, applicable legislation, and human rights, social and ethical concerns. In this way, sustainable companies must foresee all possible negative impacts and collaborate with all stakeholders to create value for both shareholders and society in general (European Commission, 2011). In *Signaling Positive Corporate Social Performance: An Event Study of Family-Friendly Firms* (2011), Ray Jones and Audrey J. Murrell demonstrated that CSP and companies' commitment to social initiatives can be used as a performance indicator (Carroll, 2008).

The same year, Porter and Kramer published *Creating Shared Value* in which they recognized that, since business activity and society are connected, community well-being and business success are linked too (Porter & Kramer, 2011). In this way, long-term competition is guided by the ability to create a shared value (CSV) that can be achieved by "identifying and expanding the connections between societal and eco-nomic progress" (Porter & Kramer, 2011, p. 6) and complying with laws and ethical standards (Porter & Kramer, 2011). Porter and Kramer emphasized that shared value could bring long-term competitiveness based on innovation and growth (Porter & Kramer, 2011). In this way, the authors recommended, companies could create social and economic value by exploiting environmental resources (Porter & Kramer, 2011). They also specified that the shared value created by companies should be viewed as an increase in overall social and economic value and not as value redistributed by the company in society (Porter & Kramer, 2011). Furthermore, they declared that "shared value (CSV) should supersede corporate social responsibility (CSR) in guiding the investments of companies in their communities" (Porter & Kramer, 2011, p. 16) and

"CSR programs focus mostly on reputation and have only a limited connection to the business, making them hard to justify and maintain over the long run. In contrast, CSV is integral to a company's profitability and competitive position" (Porter & Kramer, 2011, p. 16). This means that long-term success must be based on a company's ability and on their social responsibility, thus generating shared value for both the company and society. Therefore, firms and society must cooperate to create shared value because they influence each other (Porter & Kramer, 2011). In fact, according to Porter and Kramer, negative impacts on society inevitably affect a company because the community will act against the business (Porter & Kramer, 2011). The authors criticized how companies use CSR, claiming that the strategies and activities reveal a short-term, rather than a long-term, perspective (Porter & Kramer, 2011). In 2012, Gazzola and Mella declared that companies should consider social responsibility both internally and externally (Gazzola & Mella, 2012). From an external point of view, corporations should consider the following external stakeholder areas:

• *Environmental concerns*: Considering the impacts produced on the environment on a global level, because their actions generate a wider impact than the areas in which they conduct their business
• *Human rights*: Complying with the laws related to human rights and environmental protection and adopting codes of conduct for their employees
• *Local communities*: Businesses and local communities influence each other; corporations can benefit from the stability and prosperity of the community in which they operate and, at the same time, create job opportunities for the community
• *Suppliers and commercial partnerships*: Considering how responsible social behavior of their suppliers can affect the firm's image

On the other hand, from an internal point of view, companies should consider the following (Gazzola & Mella, 2012):

• Adapting to the changes inside the organization by limiting the number of layoffs and meeting the expectations and needs of all interested parties
• Improving health and safety in the workplace
• Refining human resource management by developing measures that meet the needs of employees (such as equal pay, career prospects, and flexible working hours)
• Managing the effects on natural resources and the environment by undertaking actions that create shared value for the company and the environment

The authors also declared that CSR makes it necessary to engage in ethical behaviors based on respect for collaborators, society, and the environment (Gazzola & Mella, 2012). It requires companies to operate following the fairness and transparency principles and to respect fundamental rights (Gazzola & Mella, 2012; Ferioli, 2022b). In 2015, the United Nations' Sustainable Development Goals (SDGs) were developed following the identification of many of these needs as universal (Sachs, 2012). This topic will be deeply discussed in the following chapter. In recent decades, value systems have evolved, making CSR a mainstream topic (Gazzola, 2012c; Lyon et al., 2018). According to Nave and Ferreira (2019), the four most addressed topics in the literature related to contemporary theories are as follows (Nave & Ferreira, 2019):

1 Entrepreneurial power and the need to use it responsibly
2 Ethical policies for social well-being
3 The achievement of objectives to bring long-term profits
4 The requirement to integrate social needs

Today, people are more willing to purchase sustainable products and services from companies that have ethical, social, and environmental values (Joshi & Rahman, 2015; Kantar, 2020). In their *Special Eurobarometer 501: Attitudes of European Citizens Towards the Environment* report, the European Commission (EC) presented the results of a public opinion poll on environmental issues that was conducted in 28 European member states from December 6 to 19, 2019. The results reveal that 94% of the respondents consider environmental protection "important to them personally" and 53% "very important" (Kantar, 2020). Climate change (53%), the growing amount of waste (46%), and air pollution (46%) were identified as the principal environmental issues (Kantar, 2020). Furthermore, the respondents agreed that environmental problems will be reduced by changing their consumption habits (33%) and by altering production and trade methodologies (31%) (Kantar, 2020). Events such as the globalization of markets, changes in consumers' propensity to buy, and multiple environmental disasters have made CSR crucial to companies' long-term survival (Gazzola, 2012c). Thus, planning socially responsible goals and actions is a leading task for managers and policymakers in all industries (Meuer et al., 2020). Furthermore, the need to engage in activities and define strategies that integrate social, ethical, and environmental issues into companies' economic and financial activities has increased (TBL approach), allowing companies to operate as open social systems (Gazzola, 2012a, 2012c; Lopez, 2020). The concept of open social systems implies that society and companies can influence each other. The former generates value for shareholders and society in general by considering society's needs as the basis of their economic activity (Gazzola, 2012a, 2012c; Meo Colombo, 2021). On the other hand, society affects business activities by requiring greater transparency or by boycotting businesses that play a role in environmental pollution (Gazzola, 2012c; Meo Colombo, 2021). In this way, to generate and maintain a competitive advantage in the long term, companies need to understand how to be sustainable and how to implement socially responsible actions and strategies in their businesses (Nave & Ferreira, 2019; Lopez, 2020).

2.2.9 *The need for sustainable actions and greater transparency standards*

The pressures exerted by civil society have made it fundamental for businesses to undertake sincere sustainability activities and communicate to stakeholders about all of their impacts on society and the environment (Gazzola, 2012a; Lyon et al., 2018; Nave & Ferreira, 2019). By disclosing their sustainability results and limits, corporations meet their stakeholders' expectations and generate sustainable value, helping them to achieve a better reputation (Morsing & Schultz, 2006; Gazzola, 2012a). In the literature, stakeholder theory supporters argue that these factors ensure satisfactory levels of profitability and that social communication requires the adoption of a more conscious approach such as TBL (Pedrini, 2012; Gazzola, 2012a; Ağan et al., 2016). Transparent social communication represents a new challenge because it is crucial for maintaining legitimacy (Gazzola 2012a). In addition, it requires sophisticated communication strategies and greater transparency standards (Morsing & Schultz, 2006; Romolini et al., 2014; Gazzola et al., 2020; Tsalis et al., 2020; Threlfall et al., 2020). Moreover, government and corporate culture influence the way companies manage their relationships with stakeholders (Romolini et al., 2014; Gazzola et al., 2020). CSR must be viewed as a long-term investment and an opportunity to be competitive and to survive in the long term (Gazzola, 2012c). However, there is a risk that companies will adopt greenwashing strategies as a marketing tool by engaging in socially responsible activities only to improve their image and to remain competitive (Gazzola, 2012c; Romolini et al., 2014; Burger-Helmchen & Siegel, 2020). In fact, they could publish only information related to those policy effects that contribute to generate a positive image (Gazzola & Mella, 2012). Nevertheless, it is likely that they will only benefit from this behavior in the short term because consumers tend to punish insincere sustainable actions (Gazzola, 2012c; Gazzola & Mella, 2012; Nave & Ferreira, 2019; Ferioli, 2022b). For this reason, sincere social communication is fundamental for companies, and it is linked to the concept of corporate hypocrisy defined by Tillmann Wagner, Richard J. Lutz, and Barton A. Weitz as the "belief that a company claims to be something it is not" (Nave & Ferreira, 2019, p. 887).

2.2.10 *The impact of the pandemic on the CSR concept*

In 2019, the first case of SARS-CoV-2 (COVID-19) was discovered (Il Sole 24 Ore, 2021). Companies had to serve their customers with essential services, face late payments, and deal with canceled orders, all while their freedom to fire employees was limited by the government (Brown, 2021; Crane & Matten, 2021). The COVID-19 pandemic has created unprecedented and very strong pressures on business. Thus, the pandemic had a significant impact on the concept of CSR and the idea of companies' social obligations because it increased inequalities (Crane & Matten, 2021; Pelikánová et al., 2021). By studying female workers in the garment industry, Brown proved that supply chains' socially responsible programs were not designed to improve illegal and abusive conditions. Therefore, they didn't improve employees' working conditions (Brown, 2021). According to Radka M. Pelikánová, Tereza Němečková, and Robert K. MacGregor, COVID-19 has been perceived by some companies as an opportunity to adopt greenwashing practices or to rebuild their production portfolio and as a threat to passively survive (Pelikánová et al., 2021). In fact, some companies encountered difficulties in the pandemic and adopted greenwashing practices without actively engaging in socially responsible activities. But many companies have understood that, to meet the need of the public that ask for CSR, they need to rethink to their CSR strategy. This allows the companies to afford the crisis and to do what the public expect from them (Carroll, 2021).

The pandemic challenged businesses' ability to produce goods and services that meet society's needs. To survive in the post-pandemic period, considering the climate change, the ecosystem in trouble, the increment of the population, and the depletion of the resources highlight the necessity to develop new business models that are more sustainable than the traditional one to meet social objectives and needs (Crane & Matten, 2021; Ferioli, 2022a). It's necessary to align the CSR efforts with the need of all stakeholders. The CSR requires a long-term vision considering the real short-term pressures to recoup costs and react to new challenges.

References

Ağan, Y., Kuzey, C., Acar, M.F., & Açıkgöz, A. (2016). The relationships between corporate social responsibility, environmental supplier development, and firm performance. *Journal of Cleaner Production, 112*, 1872–1881. 10.1016/j.jclepro.2014.08.090

Agudelo, M.A., Jóhannsdóttir, L., & Davídsdóttir, B. (2019). A literature review of the history and evolution of corporate social responsibility. *International Journal of Corporate Social Responsibility, 4*(1), 1–23. 10.1186/s40991-018-0039-y

Arru, B., & Ruggieri, M. (2016). I benefici della Corporate Social Responsibility nella creazione di valore sostenibile: il ruolo delle risorse di competenza e del capitale reputazionale. *Economia Aziendale Online, 7*(1), 17–41. 10.6092/203 8-5498/7.1.17-41

Brown, G.D. (2021). Women garment workers face huge inequities in global supply chain factories made worse by COVID-19. *New Solutions: A Journal of Environmental and Occupational Health Policy, 31*(2), 113–124. 10.1177/10482 911211011605

Burger-Helmchen, T., & Siegel, E.J. (2020). Some thoughts on CSR in relation to B Corp labels. *Entrepreneurship Research Journal, 10*(4). 10.1515/erj-2020-0231

Burke, L., & Logsdon, J.M. (1996). How corporate social responsibility pays off. *Long Range Planning, 29*(4), 495–502. 10.1016/0024-6301(96)00041-6

Carroll, A.B. (1979). A three-dimensional conceptual model of corporate performance. *Academy of Management Review, 4*(4), 497–505. 10.5465/amr.1 979.4498296

Carroll, A.B. (1991). The pyramid of corporate social responsibility: Toward the moral management of organizational stakeholders. *Business Horizons, 34*(4), 39–48.

Carroll, A.B. (1999). Corporate social responsibility: Evolution of a definitional construct. *Business & Society, 38*(3), 268–295. 10.1177/000765039903800303

Carroll, A.B. (2008). A history of corporate social responsibility: Concepts and practices. *The Oxford Handbook of Corporate Social Responsibility, 1.* 10.1093/oxfordhb/9780199211593.003.0002

Carroll, A.B. (2021). Corporate social responsibility (CSR) and the COVID-19 pandemic: Organizational and managerial implications. *Journal of Strategy and Management, 14*(3), 315–330. 10.1108/JSMA-07-2021-0145

Commission of the European Communities. (2001). Green paper: Promoting a European framework for Corporate Social Responsibility. *Commission of the European Communities.*

Crane, A., & Matten, D. (2021). COVID-19 and the future of CSR research. *Journal of Management Studies, 58*(1), 280. 10.1111/joms.12642

Dahlsrud, A. (2008). How corporate social responsibility is defined: An analysis of 37 definitions. *Corporate Social Responsibility and Environmental Management, 15*(1), 1–13. 10.1002/csr.132

Davis, K. (1960). Can business afford to ignore social responsibilities? *California Management Review, 2*(3), 70–76. 10.2307/41166246

European Commission. (2011). Communication from the commission to the European parliament, the council, the European economic and social committee and the committee of the regions: A renewed EU strategy 2011–14 for Corporate Social Responsibility. *European Commission.*

Evans, W.R., Haden, S.S.P., Clayton, R.W., & Novicevic, M.M. (2013). History-of-management-thought about social responsibility. *Journal of Management History, 19*(1), 8–32. 10.1108/17511341311286150

Feng, P., & Ngai, C.S.B. (2020). Doing more on the corporate sustainability front: A longitudinal analysis of CSR reporting of global fashion companies. *Sustainability, 12*(6), 2477. 10.3390/su12062477

Ferioli, M. (2022a). B Corp: Un Nuovo Modello di Business per la Mobilità Sostenibile. Il Caso del Gruppo Maganetti. *Economia Aziendale Online, 13*(1), 53–73. 10.13132/2038-5498/13.1.53-73.

Ferioli, M. (2022b). Sustainability report as a non-financial disclosure tool for B-Corps: Analysis of the Italian fashion industry. *Economia Aziendale Online*, *13*(3), 459–478. 10.13132/2038-5498/13.3.459-478

Frederick, W.C. (1994). From CSR1 to CSR2: The maturing of business-and-society thought. *Business & Society*, *33*(2), 150–164. 10.1177/000765039403300202

Freeman, R.E., & Reed, D.L. (1983). Stockholders and stakeholders: A new perspective on corporate governance. *California Management Review*, *25*(3), 88–106. 10.2307/41165018

Friedman, M. (1962). *Capitalism and freedom*. University of Chicago Press.

Friedman, M. (1970, September 13). A Friedman doctrine: The social responsibility of business is to increase its profits. *The New York Times*. https://www.nytimes.com/1970/09/13/archives/a-friedman-doctrine-the-social-responsibility-of-business-is-to.html

Gazzola, P. (2012a). CSR e reputazione nella creazione di valore sostenibile. *Economia Aziendale Online*, *2*, 27–45. 10.13132/2038-5498/2006.2.27-45

Gazzola, P. (2012b). La comunicazione sociale nella creazione di valore sostenibile. *Economia Aziendale Online*, *2*, 11–24. 10.13132/2038-5498/2005.2.11-24

Gazzola, P. (2012c). CSR per scelta o per necessità? *Maggioli*.

Gazzola, P., & Mella, P. (2012). Corporate performance and corporate social responsibility (CSR): A necessary choice? *Economia Aziendale Online*, *3*, 1–22. 10.13132/2038-5498/2006.3.1-22

Gazzola, Patrizia, Pezzetti, Roberta, Amelio, Stefano, & Grechi, Daniele (2020). Non-Financial Information Disclosure in Italian Public Interest Companies: A Sustainability Reporting Perspective. *Sustainability*, 12(15), 6063, 1–16. 10.3390/su12156063.

Hoffman, R.C. (2007). Corporate social responsibility in the 1920s: An institutional perspective. *Journal of Management History*, *13*(1), 55–73. 10.1108/17511340710715179

Husted, B.W. (2000). A contingency theory of corporate social performance. *Business & Society*, *39*(1), 24–48. 10.1177/000765030003900104

Il Sole 24 Ore. (2021, November). Cose che noi umani. https://lab24.ilsole24ore.com/storia-coronavirus/

Jones, T.M. (1980). Corporate social responsibility revisited, redefined. *California Management Review*, *22*(3), 59–67. 10.2307/41164877

Joshi, Y., & Rahman, Z. (2015). Factors affecting green purchase behaviour and future research directions. *International Strategic Management Review*, *3*(1–2), 128–143. 10.1016/j.ism.2015.04.001

Kantar. (2020). *Special Eurobarometer 501: Attitudes of European citizens towards the environment*. European Union.

Kotler, P., & Lee, N. (2005). *Corporate Social Responsibility: Doing the most good for your company and your cause*. John Wiley & Sons.

Kreps, T.J. (1962). Measurement of the social performance of business. *The Annals of the American Academy of Political and Social Science*, *343*, 20–31. 10.1177/000271626234300104

Lantos, G.P. (2001). The boundaries of strategic corporate social responsibility. *Journal of Consumer Marketing*, *18*(7), 595–632. 10.1108/07363760110410281

44   *Corporate social responsibility*

Lee, M.D.P. (2008). A review of the theories of corporate social responsibility: Its evolutionary path and the road ahead. *International Journal of Management Reviews, 10*(1), 53–73. 10.1111/j.1468-2370.2007.00226.x

Lopez, B. (2020). Connecting business and sustainable development goals in Spain. *Marketing Intelligence & Planning, 38*(5), 573–585. 10.1108/MIP-08-201 8-0367

Lyon, T.P., Delmas, M.A., Maxwell, J.W., Bansal, T.P., Chiroleu-Assouline, M., Crifo, P., Durand, R., Gond, J.-P., King, A., Lenox, M., Toffel, M., Vogel, D., & Wijen, F. (2018). CSR needs CPR: Corporate sustainability and politics. *California Management Review, 60*(4), 5–24. 10.1177/0008125618778854

Mazurkiewicz, P. (2004). Corporate environmental responsibility: Is a common CSR framework possible? *World Bank, 2*, 1–18.

Meo Colombo, C. (2021). "Organization." A multi facet concept. *Economia Aziendale Online, 12*(4), 487–506. 10.13132/2038-5498/12.4.487-506

Meuer, J., Koelbel, J., & Hoffmann, V. H. (2020). On the nature of corporate sustainability. *Organization & Environment, 33*(3), 319–341. 10.1177/108602661 9850180

Mitchell, R.K., Agle, B.R., & Wood, D.J. (1997). Toward a theory of stakeholder identification and salience: Defining the principle of who and what really counts. *Academy of Management Review, 22*(4), 853–886. 10.5465/amr.1 997.9711022105

Morsing, M., & Schultz, M. (2006). Corporate social responsibility communication: Stakeholder information, response and involvement strategies. *Business ethics: A European Review, 15*(4), 323–338. 10.1111/j.1467-8608.2006.00460.x

Nave, A., & Ferreira, J. (2019) Corporate social responsibility strategies: Past research and future challenge. *Corporate Social Responsibility and Environmental Management, 26*(4), 885–901. 10.1002/csr.1729

Pedrini, M. (2012). I bilanci di sostenibilità e delle risorse intangibili: il processo di integrazione nelle aziende italiane. *Economia Aziendale Online, 1*, 117–146. 10.13132/2038-5498/2007.1.117-146

Pelikánová, R.M., Němečková, T., & MacGregor, R.K. (2021). CSR statements in international and czech luxury fashion industry at the onset and during the COVID-19 pandemic—slowing down the fast fashion business? *Sustainability, 13*(7), 1–19, 3715. 10.3390/su13073715

Perrini, F. (2006). Book review of corporate social responsibility: Doing the most good for your company and your cause by Philip Kotler and Nancy Lee. *Academy of Management Perspectives, 20*(2), 90–93.

Phillips, R. (2003). *Stakeholder theory and organizational ethics.* Berrett-Koehler Publishers.

Porter, M.E., & Kramer, M.R. (2006). Strategy and society: The link between corporate social responsibility and competitive advantage. *Harvard Business Review, 84*(12), 78–92.

Porter, M.E., & Kramer, M.R. (2011). The big idea: Creating shared value. *Harvard Business Review, 89*, 2–17.

Romolini, A., Fissi, S., & Gori, E. (2014). Scoring CSR reporting in listed companies—Evidence from Italian best practices. *Corporate Social Responsibility and Environmental Management, 21*(2), 65–81. 10.1002/ csr.1299

Sachs J.D. (2012). From millennium development goals to sustainable development goals. *The Lancet*, *379*(9832), 2206–2211. 10.1016/S0140-6736(12)60685-0

Selznick, P. (1957). *Leadership in administration*. University Press Books.

Sethi, S.P. (1975). Dimensions of corporate social performance: An analytical
framework. *California Management Review*, *17*(3), 58–64. 10.2307/41162149

Smith, N.C. (2001). Changes in corporate practices in response to public interest
advocacy and actions. In *Handbook of marketing and society* (pp. 140–161).
London, Thousand Oaks: Sage Publications.

Threlfall, R., King, A., Shulman, J., & Bartels, W. (2020). The time has come: The
KPMG survey of sustainability reporting. *KPMG*, 1–63.

Tsalis, T.A., Malamateniou, K.E., Koulouriotis, D., & Nikolaou, I.E. (2020).
New challenges for corporate sustainability reporting: United Nations' 2030
Agenda for sustainable development and the sustainable development goals.
Corporate Social Responsibility and Environmental Management, *27*(4),
1617–1629. 10.1002/csr.1910

Van Marrewijk, M. (2003). Concepts and definitions of CSR and corporate
sustainability: Between agency and communion. *Journal of Business Ethics*,
44(2), 95–105. https://www.jstor.org/stable/25075020

Ward H. (2004). Public sector roles in strengthening corporate social responsibility: Taking stock. Washington, DC: World Bank.

WBCSD. (1998, September 6–8). Stakeholder dialogue on CSR. The Nederlands.
https://www.wbcsd.org

3 Non-financial reporting, integrated reporting, and sustainability performance

3.1 Non-financial disclosure and environmental, social, and governance principles

Parallel with the evolution of shareholder and stakeholder management approaches, it is possible to distinguish three different phases of the evolution of non-financial reporting:

1 Before the 1980s, some preliminary work and legislation activities were undertaken with the aim of standardizing the reporting, at least at the national level.
2 During the 1980s, there was decreasing interest in social reporting. Particularly, organizations did not make following the theoretical framework a robust practice.
3 From the 1990s to the present, there was a renaissance in terms of businesses, institutions, and economic organizations recognizing the importance of guidelines and standardized models for non-financial reporting (Dragu & Tudor-Tiron, 2013).

The increasing care regarding organizations' socially responsible behavior led to the development of models and standards for non-financial reporting that became accepted globally. Such models give organizations the opportunity to report their non-financial initiatives and results and share them with all stakeholders, thus creating shared value.

The generic terms "non-financial reporting" or "sustainable reporting" generally include other terms that are increasingly known today, for example:

• Corporate social responsibility (CSR) reporting
• Environment, social, and governance (ESG) reporting
• Global Reporting Initiative (GRI)
• Integrated reporting (IR)

DOI: 10.4324/9781003388470-4

Increasing pressure from consumers and public opinion led organizations to report and communicate their corporate socially responsible behavior and activity. In addition, the pressure exerted by the Organization for Economic Co-Cperation and Development (OECD) and the European Union (EU), as well as stakeholders' attention to sustainable activities, generated the need for companies to disclose information regarding how they achieve their social purpose and what impact they have on society and the environment (Morsing & Schultz, 2006; IIRC, 2011; Romolini et al., 2014; Joshi & Rahman, 2015; Nave & Ferreira, 2019; Gazzola et al., 2020). For this reason, companies must adopt a more conscious approach that is in line with the triple bottom line (TBL), which merges the social and environmental dimensions with the economic one (Elkington, 1997; Gazzola, 2012a; Pedrini, 2012; Alhaddi, 2015). ESG principles are set by analysts who identify relevant and specific issues within different industries, sectors, and companies. They are used by investors to evaluate and select investments based on company policies. These principles encourage companies to act responsibly and seek to ensure that companies are respectful of the environment and society and are led by responsible managers. ESG is based on the following three key dimensions (Amel-Zadeh & Serafeim, 2018):

1 The environmental dimension concerns greenhouse gas emissions, waste management, and compliance with environmental regulations. It includes company climate policies relating to energy use, waste management, polluting emissions, conservation of natural resources, and treatment of animals. ESG helps investors assess the environmental risks a company may face and understand its ability to manage those risks.
2 The social dimension concerns relations with internal and external stakeholders. Investors look for companies that promote socially conscious and ethical issues, including community care, diversity, inclusion, and the fight against gender, sexual, and racial discrimination.
3 The governance dimension concerns the use of transparent accounting methods, integrity, and responsible management practices toward shareholders. Corporate governance strategies are a fundamental element for the proper functioning of a sustainable organization. For example, investors require companies to avoid conflicts of interest when selecting board members and senior management.

Today, corporate governance and CSR are key elements in growing citizens' trust as well as contributing factors to businesses' competitiveness. Well-managed organizations can contribute significantly to the achievement of the ambitious objectives of sustainable growth.

Therefore, corporate governance must balance the interests of different stakeholders, and identifying the needs and expectations of stakeholders must be included in the decision-making process. Corporate leadership must introduce clear sustainability objectives into the strategy and communicate them throughout the organization, translating their vision into action. Managing the transformation toward sustainability must include integrating a "sustainability culture" within the organization so that it becomes a fundamental value of the organization.

To establish relationships of trust with stakeholders, organizations need to develop social communication. This is a requirement for companies because stakeholders are increasingly interested in knowing how companies contribute to the environment and the well-being of society, and social communication is the best way for companies to communicate information about these features of their work (Romolini et al., 2014; Joshi & Rahman, 2015; Lee & Lee, 2018; Nave & Ferreira, 2019). However, doing so requires a more conscious approach that merges the social and environmental dimensions with the economic one (Gazzola, 2012a; Pedrini, 2012; Ferioli, 2022a). This means that companies must disclose financial and non-financial information. The latter includes some topics such as their contributions to improving waste treatment, pollution, climate change, health, employee safety, and the use of resources and energy (Gazzola et al., 2020). In this way, social communication bridges the gap generated by market symmetries to increase companies' economic value, maintain their corporate legitimacy, and mitigate legislative pressures from social and political stakeholders (Gazzola, 2012a; Romolini et al., 2014; Gazzola et al., 2020; Ferioli et al., 2021). Furthermore, it allows companies to meet their stakeholders' expectations and obtain a better reputation to generate sustainable financial, social, and environmental value (Morsing & Schultz, 2006; Gazzola, 2012a; Ağan et al., 2016; Ferioli, 2022b). Social communication represents a new challenge for companies because it requires increased transparency and more sophisticated strategies than those employed in the past (Morsing & Schultz, 2006; Romolini et al., 2014; Gazzola et al., 2020; Threlfall et al., 2020; Tsalis et al., 2020). Furthermore, corporate culture and governments influence the way companies manage their relationships with stakeholders (Romolini et al., 2014; Gazzola et al., 2020).

Companies are increasingly called to share their success by disclosing the sustainability results they achieve through the non-financial statement (NFS) (also called a sustainability report) (Wray, 2015). This document combines accounting, social, environmental, and ethical information and allows companies to pursue and respond to internal and external objectives and analyses (Brogonzoli, 2005).

3.2 The development of non-financial reports

Reporting requirements have evolved differently in various jurisdictions, increasing the compliance burden for companies (IIRC, 2011). In 2020, KPMG[1] analyzed how social reporting has changed in the largest companies in the world (Threlfall et al., 2020). The analysis, which represents the most extensive of its kind, considered two samples of companies. The first sample (N100) represents the top 100 companies by revenue in every 52 countries and jurisdictions (5,200 companies). The second sample (G250) is made up of the 250 largest firms by revenue according to the 2019 Fortune 500 ranking. Sustainability reporting for N100 companies (80%) is growing worldwide (+5% from 2017), while the G250's rate (96%) differs slightly over the years because the companies in the sample change (Threlfall et al., 2020). The Americas have the highest reporting rate (90%), followed by Asia Pacific (84%), Europe (77%), and the Middle East & Africa (59%) (Threlfall et al., 2020). According to the authors, Western European rates grew slower than Eastern ones in the last three years because Eastern European governments were slower to apply the European Directive on non-financial reporting (Threlfall et al., 2020). In Italy, the reporting rate (86%) has gained +6 points since 2017 (Threlfall et al., 2020). Of course, it must be noted that the KPMG analysis only considers large companies, which suggests that the results may make some countries look better than others in terms of sustainability reporting simply because more large companies are housed there. According to Istituto Nazionale di Statistica (ISTAT),[2] 94.9% of the Italian territory are small companies, which employ 43.7% of the total employees (Istituto Nazionale di Statistica (ISTAT), 2020). This means that the reporting rate that KPMG assigned to Italy only reflects a small portion of Italian companies. Despite this, it is worth including this analysis here, as the sample of companies that we will analyze also includes listed companies.

Over the years, it has become necessary to develop minimum levels of disclosure (Romolini et al., 2014). For instance, European countries have introduced regulations that force companies to disclose non-financial information (Gazzola et al., 2020). On November 15, 2014, Directive 2014/95/EU, concerning the reporting of non-financial information, was published in the *Official Journal of the European Union* (Gazzola et al., 2020). The directive was aimed at improving the accountability and transparency of businesses. It introduced the obligation for public interest companies[3] with more than 500 workers to disclose non-financial information (Directive 2014/95/EU of the European Parliament and of the Council). Specifically, the directive requires companies to publish company policies, performance indicators, and risks regarding the following aspects of their business:

- Personnel
- Respect for human rights
- Social and environmental
- Fight against active and passive corruption

Furthermore, if a company does not have a policy regarding one of these four aspects, it must disclose the reasons for this lack (Directive 2014/95/EU of the European Parliament and of the Council). In February 2020, the European Commission decided to revise Directive 2014/95/EU (to date, that revision is still underway) (Amelio et al., 2021). In 2016, thanks to Legislative Decree No. 254/2016, Italy implemented Directive 2014/95/EU. The Legislative Decree introduced the obligation to publish annual non-financial statements that contain information related to the company's sustainable actions and policies (Gazzola et al., 2020). The Legislative Decree is applied to public interest entities who have exceeded one of the following limits:

- More than 500 employees on average during the year
- Total balance sheet of €20 million
- Total net revenues of 40 million euros from sales and services

Specifically, Article 3 imposes on managers the responsibility of ensuring that their NFS at least contains information regarding:

> the use of energy and water resources; greenhouse gas emissions and polluting emissions into the atmosphere; the impact on the environment as well as on health and safety, associated with risk factors or other relevant environmental and health risk factors; social and personnel management aspects, including actions taken to ensure gender equality, measures to implement the conventions of international and supranational organizations on the matter, and the ways in which dialogue with social partners is carried out; respect for human rights, the measures taken to prevent violations, as well as the actions taken to prevent discriminatory attitudes and actions; fight against corruption, both active and passive, with an indication of the tools adopted for this purpose.
>
> (Gazzola et al., 2020, p. 4; Legislative Decree No. 254/2016)

Article 5 establishes that an NFS can either be inside the management report, in a specific section marked as "NFS," or in a separate report (also marked with "NFS") (Legislative Decree No. 254/2016).

After the approval of Legislative Decree No. 254/2016, Deloitte[4] decided to start a National Observatory on non-financial reporting (2018) to analyze how Italian companies communicate social responsibility. The results concerned the fiscal year 2016. The sample was composed of 194 companies, 119 of which were listed companies, of which 31 belonged to the FTSE MIB index, and 44 were non-listed. Most (142) of the companies belonged to non-financial sectors, while 52 were from the financial sector. From Deloitte's analysis, it emerged that the introduction of Legislative Decree No. 254/2016 led to the development of the NFS in Italian companies (Amelio et al., 2018). Fifty-seven percent of companies had never published an NFS before 2016. According to Albareda et al. (2006), the government and public policy are the drivers of CSR in Italy (Romolini et al., 2014). That means that companies do not approach CSR as a strategic corporate decision; they use it to improve their corporate image and relations with local communities (Romolini et al., 2014). Monda and Botti (2021) showed that lack of communication ineffectiveness and lack of interest in green activities have led to CSR behaviors having little influence on customers' opinions about companies in some sectors (Monda & Botti, 2021).

In the years following the approval of Legislative Decree No. 254/2016, numerous regulations and initiatives have been published to increase the requirements of companies' transparency toward stakeholders. In June 2019, the European Commission published the *Guidelines on Reporting on Climate Information*, which recommended that businesses integrate more information about finance and climate change impacts into NFS (Amelio et al., 2021). Between June and September 2019, two legally non-binding documents were published to increase the transparency of companies on aspects related to sustainability: the *EU Green Bond Standard* and the *Report on Climate Benchmarks and Benchmarks' ESG Disclosures* (Amelio et al., 2021). Article 8 of the EU regulation 2020/852 introduced more transparency requirements too (Amelio et al., 2021). It established that, following the adoption of the European Taxonomy, companies must declare how their activities can be considered environmentally sustainable (Amelio et al., 2021). Specifically, the regulation requires non-financial companies to declare their share of turnover from sustainable products or services and their share of operating and capital account expenses relating to sustainable economic activities (Amelio et al., 2021).

As previously mentioned, Article 5 of the Legislative Decree No. 254/2016 establishes that NFS can either be inside the management report or in a separate document (Legislative Decree No. 254/2016). Deloitte analyzed the location of the NFS, and their results showed that 78% of companies published it as a separate document, while only 22% placed the NFS within the management report. Furthermore, among those who decided to publish the NFS as a separate report, only 12% opted to include it in their financial statements.

The idea of a unique model to present both financial and non-financial performance is gaining popularity among researchers and practitioners, giving rise to the integrated reporting framework[5] project. In November 2020, the international Integrated Reporting Council (IIRC) and the Sustainability Accounting Standards Board (SASB) announced their willingness to merge and create the Value Reporting Foundation in order to simplify the non-financial reporting system (Amelio et al., 2021).

In March 2021, Deloitte published the third edition of the National Observatory on non-financial reporting concerning an analysis carried out on the information present in the NFS of 202 Italian companies in 2019. Of the 149 listed companies in this analysis, 34 belonged to the FTSE MIB index, while 54 were non-listed (Amelio et al., 2021). Moreover, 148 companies belonged to the non-financial sectors and 54 to the financial ones (Amelio et al., 2021). The results showed that companies intend to give more importance to the communication of their non-financial performance by separating it from the management report (Amelio et al., 2021). Specifically, 84% of companies prefer to communicate non-financial information through a separate document (79% stand-alone document and 5% separate document included in the financial statement), while, compared to 2018, the number of companies that put the NFS into their management report (16%) remained the same (Amelio et al., 2021). Moreover, of the companies analyzed, 67.7% were inclined to use a qualitative approach in their NFS, while only 32% decided to adopt a quantitative approach (Amelio et al., 2021). Specifically, a qualitative approach is preferred by both companies that are obliged to provide non-financial information (non-voluntary) and those that are not (voluntary). Seventy percent of voluntary reporting companies prefer a qualitative approach (over the 30% who prefer quantitative), while 68% of non-voluntary companies prefer a qualitative approach (over the 32% who prefer quantitative) (Amelio et al., 2021). In the future, more quantitative information is expected to appear in the NFS, as measurements for objectives and performance improve (Amelio et al., 2021).

3.3 Sustainable reporting

Voluntarily disclosed information is often incomplete, inaccurate, biased, and difficult to compare (Gazzola et al., 2020). For this reason, it is necessary to adopt adequate reporting tools to communicate and evaluate companies' economic, social, and environmental aspects (Pedrini, 2012; Ferioli, 2022b). Usually, top management set the sustainability objectives. A change in the objectives leads to modifications of the company's internal processes to achieve these sustainable objectives, which become the subject of external communication.

A sustainability report is a tool that makes it possible to disclose a more exhaustive account of the social and environmental responsibility activities undertaken by a company undertakes than that offered by the company website (Ferioli, 2022b). Unlike financial statements, which are purely financial tools that are ineffective in responding to the growing demand for information from stakeholders, a sustainability report reveals the complexity of the non-monetary aspects of management (Ferioli, 2022b). Furthermore, as will be illustrated in the next chapter, a sustainability report meets the requirements imposed by law and B-Lab to B-Corps in terms of transparency (Pedrini, 2012). A sustainability report helps companies communicate the social impacts of their economic choices and socially responsible behavior and allows them to shift attention from their economic and financial value to their social and environmental value (Brogonzoli, 2005; Gazzola, 2012a, 2012b, 2012c; Gazzola & Mella, 2012; Gazzola et al., 2020). It consists of a structured document that complements the company's financial statements and contains the following:

- Quantitative information, which can be both economic and non-economic
- Qualitative information, which is often used to complete and describe the results and impacts of the company's activities (Gazzola, 2012a; Romolini et al., 2014)

A sustainability report should be created according to the following principles (Gazzola, 2012a):

- Compliance with the laws and internal policies of the company
- Responsibility for the social responsibility actions taken and any omissions
- Transparency regarding the obligation to inform stakeholders of the social and environmental impacts produced by the business activity

As a reporting tool, a sustainability report uses short-, medium-, and long-term perspectives and combines accounting information with ethical and social aspects to communicate to stakeholders how a company pursues its objectives (Brogonzoli, 2005). In order to do so, this report must contain both qualitative and quantitative information (Romolini et al., 2014). Specifically, internal analysis objectives allow the company to evaluate how sustainable its business areas and strategies have been. In this way, the report acts as a self-analysis tool to improve various management aspects (Brogonzoli, 2005). The external analysis function, on the other hand, concerns the impacts produced to allow stakeholders to evaluate whether and to what extent the activities have generated value for society and the environment. Thus, it is necessary to carefully observe changes in society. The involvement of stakeholders keeps the organization up to date regarding even subtle changes in their ecosystem's balance and helps to guide the adaptive process.

A sustainability report has a prospective function too, as it can be used to evaluate future strategies through indicators useful for comparing the sustainability objectives achieved in the various years of activity. In this way, business activity can be made more effective, and managers can evaluate and plan future improvement actions. For this reason, a sustainability report represents an evaluation tool for the following (IIRC, 2011):

• Effective allocation of resources
• Strategies and long-term viability of the business model
• The information needs of investors and other interested parties

Moreover, a sustainability report offers the advantage of communicating the company's sustainability policies and promoting a positive image of a company, thus representing a useful tool for gaining the public's trust and appreciation (Gazzola & Mella, 2012). It simplifies communication with stakeholders and provides a clear view of the value generated for society and the environment and the degree of implementation of the activities undertaken. Such reporting enables companies to show stakeholders the results of their investments that do not belong to a company's characteristic management and that are sometimes far from short-term profitability (Brogonzoli, 2005). In fact, it allows stakeholders to monitor and evaluate a company's social utility (so-called sustainability performance) or to estimate whether and how much a company's activities have been sustainable (Gazzola, 2012c). Specifically, it includes one or more thematic areas for each category of stakeholders, followed by an evaluation carried out by the managers (Brogonzoli, 2005). This makes social communication more effective, which is aimed at strengthening relations with stakeholders and promotes a positive image and demonstrating that social well-being is part of the company's objectives and is included in company policies. A sustainability report must meet the requirements of transparency and truthfulness, showing both the positive and negative effects of management in order to obtain the consensus and trust of the community (Gazzola, 2012a, 2012b). The guidelines for drafting a sustainability report recommend including a description of the company, their sustainability vision, their sustainability objectives (Romolini et al., 2014), and, if they plan to measure the social utility they produce (sustainability performance), through some indicators (Brogonzoli, 2005; Gazzola, 2012a). Companies can decide to draw up the sustainability report following the guidelines they prefer, as there are no universal principles and performance indexes to evaluate the impact produced (Romolini et al., 2014). Therefore, they may communicate using qualitative and/or quantitative information. However, using only qualitative information makes it difficult to compare and quantify the social and environmental benefit generated by different companies, as social performance is communicated with a subjective measure strongly influenced by personal perceptions (Romolini et al., 2014). For this reason, reporting requirements have evolved differently in various jurisdictions, increasing the compliance burden on companies (IIRC, 2011). Furthermore, many governments have introduced minimum standards in their legal codes (Dhanesh, 2012; Agudelo et al., 2019). The most used reporting standards are as follows:

- The Integrated Reporting Framework of the International Integrated Reporting Council (IIRC) is used when the sustainability report is integrated into the financial one.
- The principles of the Study Group for the Social Report (GBS).
- The Sustainability Reporting Guidelines of the GRI, include economic, social, and environmental aspects.

To demonstrate the two requirements and gain greater trust from stakeholders, companies can decide to certify the report through an audit. This certification attests that their report follows the guidelines for the certification. The most used international standards for auditing sustainability reports are as follows (Bianchi, 2017):

- *ISAE 3000 (Assurance Engagements Other than Audits or Reviews of Historical Financial Information)*: It is part of the ISA principles developed by the International Federation of Accountants (IFAC). It is the most used for reviewing sustainability reports.
- *Accountability 1000 (AA1000):* Introduced by the Institute of Social and Ethical Accountability, the AA1000AS (2008) assesses adherence to the AA1000 Principles of Accountability and the quality of information on sustainability performance.
- *Integrated Reporting Working Group Guidelines* were developed by the International Auditing and Assurance Standards Board (IAASB).

During the creation of a sustainability report, companies must develop dedicated tools that involve stakeholders in monitoring the sustainability of management practices (Gazzola, 2012a). For each category of stakeholders, there are one or more thematic areas that managers evaluate

(Brogonzoli, 2005). The goals of this document can be grouped into three categories: communication of the results achieved, evaluation of how the objectives have been achieved, and formulation of sustainability strategies. Specifically, it allows companies to (Gazzola, 2012b):

- Demonstrate that the policies and business objectives are aimed at creating social well-being.
- Express the corporate values and culture.
- Increase transparency to facilitate democracy.
- Promote a positive company image and strengthen relationships with stakeholders.
- Report on the social and environmental results achieved and enable a comparison with previously planned objectives.
- Show the impacts of activities on society (in terms of utility, efficiency, and legitimacy).

3.4 The GRI's sustainability reporting guidelines

The first guidelines on non-financial reporting were provided by the GRI in 2000. The Coalition for Environmentally Responsible Economies and the United Nations Environment Program created the GRI in 1997 to create a system of sustainability reporting that could be used by any type of organization and that permits the comparison of sustainability performance. To this end, it has developed the broadest reporting framework used by most of the world's organizations for performance reporting related to the TBL (Boiral & Henri, 2017).

The GRI's Sustainability Reporting Guidelines are the most used social reporting model for disclosing a company's environmental, social, and economic impacts (Romolini et al., 2014; GSSB, 2020; Threlfall et al., 2020). They are a set of interrelated standards that provide an overview of how an organization's material and related impacts are managed (GSSB, 2020). The GRI Standards were released in 2006 and updated in 2011 (Romolini et al., 2014). In September 2011, ISO (International Organization for Standardization) and GRI signed a memorandum of understanding to design a sustainability reporting standard practice (Romolini et al., 2014). The Global Sustainability Standards Board (GSSB) is currently updating the GRI Universal Standards to improve the quality and consistency of reporting (GRI). Specifically, the update concerns the following:

- Consideration of revisions to the reporting principles in GRI 101: Foundation 2016
- Consideration of revisions to the reporting model in GRI 101: Foundation 2016
- Consideration of revisions to GRI 102: General Disclosures 2016

- Integration of due diligence in GRI 103: Management Approach 2016
- Integration of human rights into the GRI Standards

The GRI Standards aim to describe an organization's positive and negative contributions to sustainable development (GSSB, 2020). They partially solve global comparability because it is possible to compare the sustainability reports of the companies that adopt these standards. The GRI Standards define the content of the sustainability report as follows:

- Completeness concerns the discussion of all those relevant issues for a correct and truthful representation of the economic, social, and environmental situation. With a complete report, stakeholders can correctly assess the company's performance.
- Materiality means that the information contained in the report must reflect the economic, social, and environmental impacts. The company must indicate which factors can influence the stakeholders' decisions and assessments.
- Stakeholder inclusiveness concerns the identification of stakeholders and how the company has responded to their expectations.
- Sustainability context means that the report must include the organization's performance in the context of sustainability.

The reporting principles define the sustainability report's content and quality (GSSB, 2020):

- *Accuracy*: The information contained in the sustainability report must be sufficiently detailed to allow for the company's performance to be assessed.
- *Balance*: The report must include both positive and negative aspects to offer a complete and impartial overview of the company's performance.
- *Clarity*: The content of the report must be accessible and understandable for all stakeholders.
- *Comparability*: The information disclosed must allow comparisons with other companies and over time.
- *Reliability*: The reporting company must disclose the information so that it can be verified.
- *Timeliness*: Information must be provided in time to allow stakeholders to make decisions.

The GRI Standards can be grouped into two macro-categories: universal and topic-specific standards (GSSB, 2020).

- Universal standards (GRI 100) are those that apply to every organization preparing a sustainability report (GSSB, 2020). Specifically, "GRI 101:

Foundation" is the starting point for using GRI Standards (GSSB, 2020). It includes requirements and specific claims (GSSB, 2020). It also defines the reporting principles for the content and quality (GSSB, 2020). "GRI 102: General Disclosures" includes contextual information about the company's profile, strategy, ethics, governance, stakeholder engagement, and reporting process (GSSB, 2020). "GRI 103: Management Approach" discloses information about the management approach for each material practice (GSSB, 2020).

• Topic-specific standards are those used to report the company's economic, environmental, and social impacts (GSSB, 2020). They include three series of standards: GRI 200 (economic topic), GRI 300 (environmental topic), GRI 400 (social topic) (GSSB, 2020).

According to their reporting needs, companies can decide to draft sustainability reports using the whole set of GRI Standards or just selected standards. If a company decides to use the whole set of standards, it must declare in the sustainability report that it is drafted "in accordance" with GRI Standards (GSSB, 2020). In this case, there are two options: core or comprehensive. The core option requires the company to disclose the "minimum information needed to understand the nature of the organization, its material topics, and related impacts, and how these are managed" (GSSB, 2020, p. 21). In addition to all of the core option's information, the comprehensive option requires disclosures of the company's strategy, ethics, integrity, and governance (GSSB, 2020).

3.5 Integrated reporting

As previously mentioned, the Legislative Decree 254/2016 establishes that sustainability reports can be separated from or integrated into financial reports (Legislative Decree 254/2016; Gazzola, 2012b; Gazzola et al., 2020). An increasing number of companies are thinking about how to communicate their commitment through an integrated reporting process. The integrated report can be considered a summary of the relevant information, both financial, from the financial statements, and non-financial. It highlights in an aggregate way how an organizations' strategy, governance, performance, and prospects create value and support business continuity. Integrated reports provide stakeholders with a single document containing all financial and non-financial information to understand the value that companies generate for shareholders and society.

Adams et al. (2020) consider the following themes of disclosure: governance, strategy, management approach, performance, and targets. A company's governance must integrate sustainable development into the companies' processes, attending to both risks and opportunities, while their strategy should maximize long-term value creation for stakeholders and a positive impact on the SDGs. Management approaches must integrate sustainable development risks and opportunities into all aspects of the organization. Finally, communication of the company's performance and progress toward targets is fundamental.

Nowadays, investors need to have a clear view of a company's strategy and risks that goes beyond the information provided in financial statements (Eccles & Klimenko, 2019). Information on non-financial risks, such as resource scarcity and social and governance dynamics, is becoming increasingly important (Atkins & Maroun, 2015).

Integrated reports allow management to understand the interconnections between financial and economic information, with the relative qualitative-quantitative (non-financial) ones. Everything a company has available to create value should be considered, including intangibles, which now represent 80% of an organization's value. This type of reporting improves existing reporting practices because it has the advantage of showing social benefits more comprehensively than traditional reporting (IIRC, 2011). Integrated reports explain how a company accesses and uses different resources (financial, human, social) and the impact that the company has on them using short-, medium-, and long-term perspectives (IIRC, 2011). The presence of these resources makes the integrated report an important evaluation tool to assess (IIRC, 2011):

- The long-term viability of an organization's business model and strategy
- The information needs of investors and other interested parties
- The effective allocation of resources

Today, organizations operate in complex internal and external environments, and this complexity influences their decision-making processes. Different stakeholders have different expectations, including interests that are competing and often divergent. Managers must consider all of these conditions and implement a comprehensive approach to planning, measurement, and reporting. Therefore, they need to use "integrated thinking" to make decisions in inclusive decision-making, management, and reporting processes, and they need to have the ability to connect different factors that affect an organization's capacity to create value not only in the short term but also over the long term (Feng et al., 2017). An organization must incorporate integrated thinking into its activities to be able to accurately communicate its ability to create value. Moreover, integrated thinking is essential to implement an effective integrated reporting process that allows the organization to prepare an integrated financial report.

Integrated reports and integrated thinking could bring several advantages (Frias-Aceituno et al., 2014) because they makes it possible to use a systemic approach in an "integrated" way. Integrated thinking guides internal corporate communication toward improvement and provides for more active involvement by all functions. It also leads to reorganized data collection and analysis integrated with appropriate financial and non-financial key performance indicators (KPIs) based on similar scopes, timescales, and metrics (Zarzycka & Krasodomska, 2021). Aligning financial and non-financial systems and processes can create a leaner organization. Having access to integrated information can help management make more informed and strategic decisions. According to Adams (2017), the following five steps can be used to align the SDGs and the integrated report:

1 Understanding the external environment
2 Identify material issues that influence value creation
3 Developing strategy
4 Integrated thinking and connectivity
5 Integrated reporting

The first step considers the SDGs' impact on an organization's capacity to create value for itself and its stakeholders. The IR Framework considers the value created directly or through stakeholder engagement. The external environment must be considered in the value-creation process. In the second step, integrated reporting identifies, evaluates, and prioritizes matters based on their capacity to affect value creation. In their approach to the SDGs, organizations need to identify, evaluate, and prioritize the sustainable development issues that maximize outcomes. The third step regards an organization's strategy. It shows how an organization manages risks and maximizes opportunities. Organizations should decide on their strategic objectives in line with the SDGs. The fourth step consists of establishing an integrated reporting process and helps organizations to make a connection between their strategy and modifications in their external environment. It's also necessary to pay attention to the evolution of stakeholder expectations and natural resource limitations because the creation of value relates to relationships with stakeholders. However, one limitation is the scarcity of natural resources. Governance guides this process. Corporate governance needs to link the business model and the strategy to changes in the external environment. They must monitor the stakeholders' expectations, technological changes, and the evolution of natural resources' stocks. The fifth step is to prepare an integrated report explaining the organization's contribution to the SDGs and their outcomes (Adams et al., 2020).

3.6 The SDGs in non-financial reporting

The new path on sustainable development issues was initiated with the international adoption of the Agenda for Sustainable Development (*Transforming Our World: The 2030 Agenda for Sustainable Development*), which represented a turning point in the global approach to sustainable development. It provides the various states with a common framework for developing appropriate national policies. Agenda 2030 is accompanied by a set of indicators that function to monitor the state of implementation (through the mechanism of Voluntary National Reviews of the High-Level Political Forum and the Annual Report on SDGs created by the UN secretariat) and to guide states toward a national framework for monitoring sustainable development policies that are as homogeneous and coherent as possible with the global framework.

Organizations have an essential role to play in helping to achieve the 17 SDGs, which are also reference objectives for evaluating an organization's contribution to sustainable development. Organizations transitioning to more sustainable business models represent a fundamental step for the SDGs' achievement. Regulations are also crucial in encouraging firms to invest in this transition (Pizzi et al., 2021). This objective can be achieved with the contribution of a reporting process that is aligned with the measurement and monitoring system used to evaluate sustainability performance as well (García-Sánchez et al., 2022). The alignment allows all organizations to define common actions by which they plan to achieve the SDGs. Organizations are encouraged to include the SDGs in non-financial reporting by progressively adopting reporting forms, such as the integrated report, which give them the opportunity to compare themselves with other organizations, both local and global.

Adopting a standard that improves comparability, transparency, and accountability enables effective information gathering, helps to share accountability and governance, and aligns decision-making and actions toward achieving meaningful and measurable global goals. Specifically, a structured reporting action concerning Agenda 2030 is a fundamental element for an organization that wants to be transparent. Social reporting moves in the direction of implementing a procedure that leads to non-financial reports that collect performance and strategies concerning the 17 SDGs (Pizzi et al., 2021). Non-financial reporting should not only integrate the SDGs but also complement them with ESG metrics in a combined way. Doing so allows organizations to have data and information on which to base their strategy, their implementation of sustainable policies, and their dialogue with stakeholders.

Notes

1 KPMG provides professional services to businesses and specializes in accounting, auditing, management consulting, tax, and legal and administrative services. It is part of the "Big Four" (KPMG, Deloitte, PricewaterhouseCoopers, and Ernst & Young) that are the four largest auditing firms worldwide.
2 ISTAT is the leading producer of public statistical research. It is part of the European Statistical System and collaborates with the other subjects of the international statistical system.
3 Public interest companies are defined in Article 18 of Legislative Decree no. 39 of January 27, 2010.

4 Deloitte is the leading consulting and auditing company in the world in terms of revenues and number of professionals. It is part of the "Big Four" (Deloitte, KPMG, PricewaterhouseCoopers, and Ernst & Young), the four largest auditing firms worldwide.
5 See: http://www.theiirc.org/

References

Adams, C.A. (2017). The Sustainable Development Goals, integrated thinking and the integrated report. *Integrated Reporting (IR)*, 1–52.
Adams, C., Druckman, P., & Picot, R. (2020). Sustainable development goals disclosure (SDGD) recommendations. Association of Chartered Certified Accountants (ACCA), Institute of Chartered Accountants of Scotland (ICAS), Chartered Accountants Australia and New Zealand (CA ANZ), the International Integrated Reporting Council (IIRC) and the World Benchmarking Alliance.
Ağan, Y., Kuzey, C., Acar, M.F., & Açıkgöz, A. (2016). The relationships between corporate social responsibility, environmental supplier development, and firm performance. *Journal of Cleaner Production, 112*, 1872–1881. 10.1016/j.jclepro.2014.08.090
Agudelo, M.A.L., Jóhannsdóttir, L., & Davídsdóttir, B. (2019). A literature review of the history and evolution of corporate social responsibility. *International Journal of Corporate Social Responsibility, 4*(1), 1–23. 10.1186/s40991-018-0039-y
Albareda, Laura, Tencati, Antonio, Lozano, Josep M., & Perrini, Francesco (2006). The government's role in promoting corporate responsibility: a comparative analysis of Italy and UK from the relational state perspective. *Corporate Governance: The international journal of business in society, 6*(4), 386–400. 10.1108/14720700610689504.
Alhaddi, H. (2015). Triple bottom line and sustainability: A literature review. *Business and Management Studies, 1*(2), 6–10. 10.11114/bms.v1i2.752
Amel-Zadeh, A., & Serafeim, G. (2018). Why and how investors use ESG information: Evidence from a global survey. *Financial Analysts Journal, 74*(3), 87–103. 10.2469/faj.v74.n3.2
Amelio, F., Demartini, M.C., Dallai, S., & Mara, F. (2021). Osservatorio Nazionale sulla Rendicontazione Non Finanziaria. Deloitte, 1–54.
Amelio, F., Perrini, F., Palumbo, M., Minichilli, A., Dallai, S., & Romito, S. (2018). Osservatorio Nazionale sulla Rendicontazione non Finanziaria ex D.Lgs. 254/2016. Deloitte and SDA Bocconi School of Management, 1–40.
Atkins, J., & Maroun, W. (2015). Integrated reporting in South Africa in 2012: Perspectives from South African institutional investors. *Meditari Accountancy Research, 23*(2), 197–221. 10.1108/MEDAR-07-2014-0047
Bianchi S (2017). Assurance del report integrato: Linee guida per laaudit secondo gli standard internazionali e italiani. *Laazienda sostenibile*, 41, 41–54.
Boiral, O., & Henri, J.F. (2017). Is sustainability performance comparable? A study of GRI reports of mining organizations. *Business & Society, 56*(2), 283–317. 10.1177/0007650315576134
Brogonzoli, L. (2005). La rendicontazione sociale. *Elemond scuola & azienda*.
Dhanesh, G.S. (2012). The view from within: Internal publics and CSR. *Journal of Communication Management, 16*(1), 39–58. 10.1108/13632541211197987

Directive 2014/95/EU of the European Parliament and of the Council of October 22nd, 2014.

Dragu, I., & Tudor-Tiron, A. (2013). New corporate reporting trends. Analysis on the evolution of integrated reporting. *Annals of the University of Oradea, Economic Science Series, 22*(1), 1221–1228.

Eccles, R.G., & Klimenko, S. (2019). The investor revolution. *Harvard Business Review, 97*(3), 106–116.

Elkington, J. (1997). The triple bottom line. *Environmental Management: Readings and Cases, 2,* 49–66.

Feng, T., Cummings, L., & Tweedie, D. (2017). Exploring integrated thinking in integrated reporting—an exploratory study in Australia. *Journal of Intellectual Capital, 18*(2), 330–353. 10.1108/JIC-06-2016-0068

Ferioli, M. (2022a). B Corp: un nuovo modello di business per la mobilità sostenibile. il caso del Gruppo Maganetti. *Economia Aziendale Online, 13*(1), 53–73. 10.13132/2038-5498/13.1.53-73

Ferioli, M. (2022b). Sustainability report as a non-financial disclosure tool for B-Corps: Analysis of the Italian fashion industry. *Economia Aziendale Online, 13*(3), 459–478. 10.13132/2038-5498/13.3.459-478

Ferioli, M., Freitas, M., & Spulber, D. (2021). The freedom to be sustainable, from the past to the future. *Geopolitical, Social Security and Freedom Journal, 4*(2), 59–79. 10.2478/gssfj-2021-0012

Frias-Aceituno, J.V., Rodríguez-Ariza, L., & Garcia-Sánchez, I.M. (2014). Explanatory factors of integrated sustainability and financial reporting. *Business Strategy and the Environment, 23*(1), 56–72. 10.1002/bse.1765

García-Sánchez, I.M., Aibar-Guzmán, B., Aibar-Guzmán, C., & Somohano-Rodríguez, F.M. (2022). The drivers of the integration of the sustainable development goals into the non-financial information system: Individual and joint analysis of their influence. *Sustainable Development, 30*(4), 513–524. 10.1002/sd.2246

Gazzola, P. (2012a). CSR e reputazione nella creazione di valore sostenibile. *Economia Aziendale Online,* (2), 27–45. 10.13132/2038-5498/2006.2.27-45

Gazzola, P. (2012b). *CSR per scelta o per necessità?* Santarcangelo di Romagna: Maggioli.

Gazzola, P. (2012c). La comunicazione sociale nella creazione di valore sostenibile. *Economia Aziendale Online,* (2), 11–24. 10.13132/2038-5498/2005.2.11-24

Gazzola, P., & Mella, P. (2012). Corporate performance and corporate social responsibility (CSR). A necessary choice? *Economia Aziendale Online,* (3), 1–22. 10.13132/2038-5498/2006.3.1-22

Gazzola, P., Pezzetti, R., Amelio, S., & Grechi, D. (2020). Non-financial information disclosure in Italian public interest companies: A sustainability reporting perspective. *Sustainability, 12*(15), 6063. 10.3390/su12156063

Global Sustainability Standards Board (GSSB). (2020). Consolidated set of GRI Sustainability Reporting Standards 2020. *Global Reporting Initiative,* pp. 5–33

GRI. Universal Standards: Setting a new global benchmark for sustainability reporting. Available at: https://www.globalreporting.org/standards/standards-development/the-review-of-the-universal-standards/

International Integrated Reporting Committee (IIRC). (2011). Towards integrated reporting—communicating value in the 21st century. *International integrated reporting committee publications*, 3–4. Available at: www.theiirc.org

Istituto Nazionale di Statistica (ISTAT). (2020). *Annuario statistico italiano*. 506.

Joshi, Y., & Rahman, R. (2015). Factors affecting green purchase behaviour and future research directions. *International Strategic Management Review, 3*(1–2), 128–143. 10.1016/j.ism.2015.04.001

Lee, J., & Lee, Y. (2018). Effects of multi-brand company's CSR activities on purchase intention through a mediating role of corporate image and brand image. *Ournal of Fashion Marketing and Management: An International Journal, 22*(3), 387–403. 10.1108/JFMM-08-2017-0087

Legislative Decree n. 254 of December 30th, (2016). It was approved by the Italian government on December 30, 2016, and implemented the EU framework on the disclosure of diversity and non-financial information (Directive 2014/95/EU of the European Parliament and of the Council of October 22, 2014, which amends the Directive 2013/34/EU).

Monda, A., & Botti, A. (2021). I rischi della Corporate Social Responsibility per le imprese etiche e lo scetticismo del consumatore green. *Corporate Governance and Research & Development Studies, 1*, 101–128. 10.3280/cgrds1-2021oa10552

Morsing, M., & Schultz, M. (2006). Corporate social responsibility communication: Stakeholder information, response and involvement strategies. *Business Ethics: A European Review, 15*(4), 323–338. 10.1111/j.1467-8608.2006.00460.x

Nave, A., & Ferreira, J. (2019). Corporate social responsibility strategies: Past research and future challenges. *Corporate Social Responsibility and Environmental Management, 26*(4), 885–901. 10.1002/csr.1729

Pedrini, M. (2012). I bilanci di sostenibilità e delle risorse intangibili: il processo di integrazione nelle aziende italiane. *Economia Aziendale Online*, (1), 117–146. 10.13132/2038-5498/2007.1.117-146

Pizzi, S., Rosati, F., & Venturelli, A. (2021). The determinants of business contribution to the 2030 Agenda: Introducing the SDG Reporting Score. *Business Strategy and the Environment, 30*(1), 404–421. 10.1111/jifm.12139

Romolini, A., Fissi, S., & Gori, E. (2014). Scoring CSR reporting in listed companies—Evidence from Italian best practices. *Corporate Social Responsibility and Environmental Management, 21*(2), 65–81. 10.1002/csr.1299

Threlfall, R., King, A., Shulman, J., & Bartels, W. (2020). The time has come: The KPMG survey of sustainability reporting. KPMG, 1–63.

Tsalis, Thomas A., Malamateniou, Kyveli E., Koulouriotis, Dimitrios, & Nikolaou, Ioannis E. (2020). New challenges for corporate sustainability reporting: United Nations' 2030 Agenda for sustainable development and the sustainable development goals. *Corporate Social Responsibility and Environmental Management, 27*(4), 1617–1629. 10.1002/csr.1910.

Wray, V. (2015). Communicating social impact. Retrieved June 25, 2016, from https://www.conference-board.org/publications/publicationdetail.cfm?publicationid=2968&centerId=1

Zarzycka, E., & Krasodomska, J. (2021). Non-financial key performance indicators: What determines the differences in the quality and quantity of the disclosures? *Journal of Applied Accounting Research, 23*(1), 139–162. 10.1108/JAAR-02-2021-0036

4 Benefit Corporations and certified B Corps' innovative business model

4.1 The Benefit Corporations' and certified B Corps' innovative model for doing business in a sustainable way

As illustrated in the previous chapters, corporate social responsibility (CSR) and social communication have become two fundamental requirements for companies to enter a market competitively and maintain a competitive advantage in the medium to long term (Gazzola et al., 2019; Ferioli et al., 2021). In fact, it is not enough to undertake socially responsible activities; it is also essential to communicate with stakeholders who are increasingly interested in knowing how companies carry out their activities (Romolini et al., 2014; Joshi & Rahman, 2015; Lee & Lee, 2018; Nave & Ferreira, 2019).

According to Bocken et al. (2015), business models can guide organizations to make changes towards sustainability. A business model shows stakeholders an organization's process of doing business and helps them to understand the organization's goals. Nowadays, it has become necessary to develop innovative business models that integrate social and environmental aspects with economic ones, especially following the pandemic (Ferioli, 2022a; Gazzola et al., 2022). Social responsibility means that companies must respect the concerns of all stakeholders in society. Environmental responsibility refers to the efficient use of resources to reduce waste and emissions. These two elements must be considered together without forgetting the economy, i.e., the need to generate a profit, create new jobs, and participate in the development of the local economy. Therefore, innovative business models should reduce negative external impacts on the natural environment and society while creating positive external effects. Combining these three elements often presents a challenge.

Benefit Corporations and B Corps are two complementary ways of thinking about an organizational business model. A Benefit Corporation is a legal identity provided for by law, while Certified B Corps are organizations that have obtained a certification by passing an assessment

DOI: 10.4324/9781003388470-5

of their sustainability and ESG performance (Gazzola et al., 2019; Burger-Helmchen & Siegel, 2020). Although these two types of companies possess distinct characteristics, they share the goal of contributing to the well-being of society. An organization can be any of the following:

- A Benefit Corporation and a Certified B Corp
- A Benefit Corporation but not a Certified B Corp
- A Certified B Corp but not a Benefit Corporation (however, in some countries, organizations have to become a Benefit Corporation if they want to keep their B Corp certification)

The B Corps' business model tries to align profit with positive social and environmental outcomes (Stubbs, 2017). In fact, Benefit Corporations and certified B Corps balance the need to generate profits with the urgency of social responsibility. In the literature, they are defined as hybrid organizations because they are placed between profit and non-profit companies (i.e., those that aim only to achieve a social benefit) (Mion & Adaui, 2020; Riolfo, 2020; Ferioli, 2022a). This business model is deemed "hybrid" because it is both innovative and sustainable.

Starting from top management, respect for the environment, diversity, and social inclusion must be fundamental to all collaborators and employees. In this way, B Corps become vehicles of renewal and transformation for each territory and community where they operate. The B Corp Certification makes it possible to measure the environmental and social impact of the organization at a given moment. However, it does not concretely represent a guarantee in the medium or long term (Honeyman & Jana, 2019). In fact, a company's management and decision-making processes can change. For this reason, a further and complementary step was taken first in the United States and, subsequently, the rest of the world. This was the creation of a new legal structure called Benefit Corporation, which is more binding than an independent certification. It integrates the company's mission within a statute, giving a greater guarantee from a long-term perspective. The first legal recognition took place in 2010 in the State of Maryland in the United States. At this time, a Benefit Corporation was identified as a "third way" between profit and non-profit, also sometimes called "for-benefit" (Bauer & Umlas, 2017).

While the economic aspect is distinct from the legislative aspect, they are complementary. On the one hand, there is a mechanism, the certification, which measures and evaluates an organization's economic, environmental, and social impact; on the other hand, the new legal designation modifies an organization's purpose, inserting environmental and social objectives alongside the economic ones.

4.2 Benefit Corporations

A Benefit Corporation is an alternative to traditional business and represents a new way of managing business and sustainability. Born in 2010 in Maryland (Gazzola et al., 2019; B Lab Europe, 2021), Benefit Corporations represent a type of enterprise driven by a purpose rather than the market (Mion & Adaui, 2020). They aim to generate profits while also meeting social and environmental objectives. Therefore, they contribute positively to society and the environment. Benefit Corporations balance the need to generate profits with the urgency of social responsibility (Gazzola et al., 2019). They can be defined as for-profit enterprises that combine Shareholder Theory (supported by Neoclassical Theory), Stakeholder Theory, and Porter and Kramer's Shared Value Creation Theory (2019). In this way, Benefit Corporations aim to generate profits and improve the well-being of society and the natural environment by reducing the negative impacts on all stakeholders (Gazzola et al., 2019; Riolfo, 2020). The social benefits derive from responsible and transparent activities that include reducing negative impacts on territories, people, cultural activities, associations, cultural heritage, and more (Riolfo, 2020). Choosing the most appropriate legal status is challenging because sustainable companies pursue both social and financial goals (Mion & Adaui, 2020). The legal form of Benefit Corporations offers the advantage of being able to preserve social objectives despite capital increases, generational transitions, stock market listings, and leadership changes. Benefit Corporations must indicate the specific objectives of common benefit they intend to pursue in their corporate purpose. Mutual benefit is accomplished by achieving positive effects and reducing negative effects for many categories of stakeholders, including people, communities, territories, the environment, cultural and social heritage, bodies and associations, and other stakeholders. To fulfill these purposes, the Benefit Corporations must be governed in such a way as to balance the interests of shareholders and the pursuit of the common benefit. Since 2014, Benefit Corporations have been controlled by the regulatory model of B Lab, which is the non-profit company that developed the B Corp Certification and created an infrastructure that allows for the coordination of all the B Corps in the network (B Lab, 2022). States can use this model as a basis to develop new legislation and introduce this type of enterprise (Gazzola et al., 2019). B Lab has created three initiatives aimed at building a legal infrastructure, building a community of Certified B Corps, and developing a rating system called the Global Impact Investing Rating System (GIIRS) (Mion & Adaui, 2020; B Lab, 2022). To date, the states that recognize Benefit Corporations are the United States of America (37 states only), Italy, Colombia, Canada, France, Ecuador, Puerto Rico, Peru, and Rwanda (Nativa, 2021; B Lab, 2022).

Benefit Corporations are part of the European Union's action plan to promote sustainable economic growth and the development of social enterprises (Riolfo, 2020; B Lab, 2022). With the approval of the Stability Law n.208 of December 28, 2015, Italy was the first European country to recognize these companies (Gazzola et al., 2019; Mion & Adaui, 2020; Nativa, 2021). This law did not introduce a new type of company, but it allowed existing companies to include financial and social objectives in their corporate purpose (Riolfo, 2020). Article 1 (para. 376–384) declares that Benefit Corporations are traditional enterprises that possess higher standards in terms of transparency, purpose, and accountability (Mion & Adaui, 2020; Mion et al., 2021). Specifically, the law declares that Benefit Corporations serve dual purpose of creating profits for shareholders and positively impacting society and environment. Paragraph 376 identifies the beneficiaries of Benefit Corporations' activities as people, entities and associations, communities, cultural and social assets and activities, the environment, and territories. They include workers, suppliers, customers, lenders, creditors, public administration, and civil society (Riolfo, 2020). Therefore, it is possible to state that it is Benefit Corporations' responsibility to generate shared value between financial and non-financial stakeholders. To do so, managers must evaluate financial performance and achieve social objectives. Finally, in terms of transparency obligations, the Stability Law requires the appointment of a manager to assess the impacts produced on society and verify that the company is complying with transparency requirements (Mion & Adaui, 2020; Mion et al., 2021). Benefit Corporations must report their impacts on society, the social objectives they have achieved, and their future sustainability strategies annually. In particular, paragraph 383 establishes that they must publish their social balance sheets on their websites.

4.3 Certified B Corps

The B Corp movement represents a hybrid conception of business that links economic value and social value. It highlights how the way of doing business has radically changed. Certified B Corps make their commitments to social value more concrete and demonstrate their attention to ethical issues to all stakeholders, which also positively influences their economic performance. B Corps are revolutionizing the way of doing business because they were developed to face this challenge (Ferioli, 2022a).

Certified B Corps aim to increase its profits while simultaneously creating a positive impact on society and the environment. They represent a solution that protects and improves the corporate mission by creating value for all stakeholders. Certified B Corps, which are independently certified companies, should not be confused with Benefit Corporations, which are companies with a new legal designation identifying a "hybrid" business model that intends to pursue and achieve both "profit" and "non-profit" objectives. The two business identities are not necessarily interdependent and equivalent. For instance, it is possible that a state may recognize Certified B Corps without having any legal apparatus for recognizing Benefit Corporations. Certified B Corps are part of the B Corps movement, a group of companies operating in multiple sectors worldwide and united by the desire to change the way business is done using their innovative vision of the concept of CSR (Burger-Helmchen & Siegel, 2020; Blasi & Sedita, 2021; Gazzola et al., 2022). Their goal is to generate positive competition in the market and allow companies to be evaluated based on the impact they produce on society and the natural environment (Gazzola et al., 2019; Burger-Helmchen & Siegel, 2020; Blasi & Sedita, 2021; Nativa, 2021). This means that they consider the expectations of all stakeholders.

Certified B Corps possess the certification developed in June 2006 by the US non-profit company B Lab (Gazzola et al., 2019; Burger-Helmchen & Siegel, 2020; Blasi & Sedita, 2021). To obtain this certification, companies must undertake an assessment process called the B Impact Assessment (BIA), which evaluates their social and environmental performance, legal responsibility, and transparency (B Impact Assessment, 2021). The certification is not a legal requirement; however, it is often used by companies to legitimize their commitment to society and the environment and influence consumers' willingness to pay a higher price for sustainable goods (Choi et al., 2012; Gazzola et al., 2020; Vu et al., 2020; Kim, 2021). All types of for-profit companies can obtain the certification, while non-profit organizations (or non-commercial organizations) are not eligible for certification. The process is free, but companies that obtain the certification have to pay an annual fee. From a practical point of view, the path to becoming a Certified B Corp is quite complex and rigorous. The certification process involves the following three essential phases:

1 Complete the Benefit Impact Assessment (BIA)
2 Validate the result with B-Lab
3 Sign the Declaration of Interdependence

During the first phase, companies must fill out a questionnaire about the organization's practices and outcomes. Their answers to the questions are used to assess their impact according to the following areas of activity: Communities, Customers, Environment, Governance, and Workers (Geerts & Dooms, 2020).

The "Communities" section evaluates the organization's contribution to the economic and social well-being of the communities in which it operates through factors such as diversity and inclusion, job creation, civic engagement and philanthropy, supply chain management, and more. It highlights the practices and activities in which the organization involves commercial partners and the local community.

The "Customers" section focuses on the relationship that the organization has with customers, including considering their expectations, requests, and needs. It evaluates the value the company creates for direct consumers of its products or services through factors such as ethical and positive marketing, product and service quality assurance, data privacy, data security, and more.

The "Environment" section analyzes the company's initiatives in terms of their adoption of environmental sustainability along the entire production chain. It refers to the activities carried out to manage or prevent environmental problems such as waste management, the efficient and effective use of energy and water, and the adoption of recycling programs or recycled products. Furthermore, this section assesses the company's overall environmental impact and management, meaning how the company manages general environmental impacts, as well as specific topics such as water use, waste disposal, sustainability, and impacts on earth and life.

The "Governance" section refers to the transparency and accountability connected with the corporate mission through factors such as the integration of social and environmental objectives in employee performance evaluation, impact reporting, transparency stakeholder engagement, and more. This section also considers the adoption of strategic choices in terms of environmental sustainability and social sustainability on behalf of stakeholders.

The "Workers" section refers to an increasingly important and central feature of organizations: people. It evaluates the company's care for its workforce by considering human resource management policies, including health, well-being, safety, career development, commitment, satisfaction, and more. Employees should be an integral part of an organization. Therefore, they must be appropriately involved. In other words, this section underlines how the organization protects and relates to its workers.

The questions on the evaluative questionnaire are both operational and motivational. A few examples are as follows (B Impact Assessment, 2022):

- *Community*: What percentage of management is composed of minorities/previously excluded populations, women, people with disabilities, and people living in low-income communities?
- *Customers*: Does the company verify the improvement of the impact on customers?

- *Environment*: Does the organization monitor and record waste generation?
- *Governance*: How are managers evaluated in writing on their performance regarding corporate, social, and environmental objectives?
- *Workers*: What is the percentage of satisfied or engaged employees based on the results of the employee satisfaction assessment of the last two years?

Completing the questionnaire allows the organization to obtain two different results at the same time. On the one hand, it verifies the company's impact of the company; on the other hand, it provides the company with important information about how to become more sustainable.

B Lab assigns a score for each area. The points assigned to each question are subject to an evaluation that varies according to the companies' geographical area, sector, and size. Finally, companies that have performed best in the categories of workers, changemakers, and governance can earn extra points. The final score is called the B Impact Score and is determined by the sum of all the scores obtained in the various categories. It can vary from a minimum of 80 to a maximum of 200 points. To date, the median score of traditional firms is 50.9 (B Impact Assessment, 2021). Therefore, Certified B Corporations have, on average, a higher level of sustainability than traditional companies (Ferioli et al., 2022). In the last phase of the BIA, B Lab provides companies with feedback to improve their social impact (Gazzola et al., 2019; Burger-Helmchen & Siegel, 2020). The result enables the organization to activate an improvement process.

The second phase starts if at least 80 points out of 200 are obtained. Organizations can ask B-Lab for verification and validation. If the result of the verification and validation process by B-Lab is positive, they can request confirmation of the self-assessment's outcome. The result is made public and divided according to each specific area.

In the third stage, the organization signs the B Corp Agreement & Declaration of Interdependence, pays their first annual fee, and can start legitimately using the "Certified B Corp" brand in its communications.

The B Corp certification is valid for three years, after which the process must be repeated (Gazzola et al., 2019) because it's necessary to take into consideration the progress and improvements that the company has actively adopted to deal with its critical aspects or weaknesses. In particular, it is necessary to update the BIA questionnaire and, consequently, to re-determine the score. Every year, 10% of the Certified B Corps worldwide are subjected to a sample check to verify that they have not adopted greenwashing practices. Additionally, each year, the 5% of global B Corps that have demonstrated the best social and environmental performance and generated the most significant impact through their activities are eligible to win the Best for the World award. The prize is awarded in five categories that reflect the areas assessed in the B Impact Assessment process: Governance, Customers, Community, Environment, and Workers (Nigri et al., 2020).

Over 450 sustainability-related certifications are available worldwide, but they often only apply to specific sectors, delimited geographical areas, or specific environmental or social problems. Unlike other sustainability-related certifications, the B Corp certification does not focus exclusively on a single issue; instead, it examines all of the impacts produced by a company. It evaluates the level of CSR without focusing only on specific aspects, such as the sustainability of raw materials or processes. Furthermore, the B Corp certification is recognized globally and is valid in various industries and sectors.

4.4 Why become a Certified B Corp?

The B Corp movement is effectively an international community that aims to use business as a positive force. According to the terms of the B Corp movement, a new role of business in society is defined in which companies compete to be "not only the best in the world but also the best for the world" (B Corporation, 2022). There are currently 6,270 Certified B Corporations in 159 different industries in 89 countries, with a total of 532,080 workers (B Corporation, 2023). Most of them reside in North America (55%), while their presence in South America (15%) and Europe (17%) is almost the same. Finally, their presence remains limited in Oceania (9%), Africa (2%), and Asia (2%) (Gazzola et al., 2019).

The pandemic period has brought about many changes. One concern was that organizations affected by the economic crisis would reduce their investments in sustainability. Instead, the B Corp Italia report highlights how in 2020, the year the pandemic took hold, Italian B Corp companies saw their turnover grow in 66% of cases, and 52% recorded an increase in employees (Certificazione B Corporation, 2021). According to data released by B Corp Italia and the Italian B Corp movement, the number of B Corp companies in Italy reached 140 in 2021, up 26% from the previous year, with a turnover of 8 billion and 15,000 employees (Certificazione B Corporation, 2021; Maccaferri, 2021). At the end of 2022, there were 200 Italian B Corp. Today, over 200,000 companies around the world measure their social and environmental performance through the B Impact Assessment tool, which was created by B Lab and is used by all B Corps.

Becoming a B Corp encourages social responsibility. By adhering to B Corp standards, which are based on transparency, companies show their customers how they are creating value. This is true especially nowadays because consumers are more and more interested in companies' sustainable activities and want to know about their social efforts. The certification process allows organizations to redefine their decision-making processes and management responsibilities. The transparency of the mission increases their attractiveness for institutional investors as well as small investors. Certified B Corps attract like-minded employees, creating a positive social change and an employee-centric culture that helps to attract and retain top talents who share the same values (Stammer, 2016). The certification process also allows companies to save on costs because they identify and eliminate needless and wasteful spending. Another significant benefit to certifying is related to reputation. Consumers are increasingly aware of the limits of the traditional business model from a sustainability perspective. They are also increasingly choosing products or services of similar quality that are valuable from a social/environmental point of view (Villela et al., 2021). Voluntarily undertaking a social and environmental commitment, especially if certified annually, stimulates the interest of consumers and other stakeholders in general. The certification process allows organizations to compare different impacts and evaluate them. Moreover, comparing themselves with other organizations that have become B Corps is useful and can be a stimulus for improvement. Through the B Impact Assessment, organizations can evaluate, compare, and improve.

On the B Lab website, it is possible to view the score assigned to each B Corp. Through the B Impact Assessment, organizations have the opportunity to identify and focus on their weak areas through adjustments and interventions in order to continue improving. This is important to underline because it is essential that organizations recognize their weaknesses and intervene accordingly, particularly if they have achieved a score of less than 80 and, consequently, fail to obtain certification (Khandker et al., 2009). In addition to self-assessment, companies have the possibility of using the quantitative results to compare with market benchmark values or those achieved by leading companies working in the same sector. Finally, B Lab verifies companies' scores by requesting information and/or documents to support the answers given in the questionnaire.

4.5 Benefit Corporations' and certified B Corps' social communication standards

Unlike traditional businesses, Benefit Corporations must meet higher transparency, purpose, and accountability standards. Their purpose is to make profits for shareholders while also generating positive impacts on society and the environment. Thus, they are responsible for creating shared value between financial and non-financial stakeholders. Some countries, like Italy, require Benefit Corporations to write an annual report that is included with their financial statements in which they detail their pursuit of common benefits. In fact, Benefit Corporations are required by law to share an annual report with their stakeholders that details their ability to create value for society. The report must clearly represent the company's objectives, results, and impacts.

These organizations evaluate, report, and make public their results and impacts on society in a structured and constant way over time (Nigri et al., 2017). Reporting is a company's leading tool for communicating with its current and potential stakeholders. Moreover, it enables companies to disseminate fundamental information and maintain good relations with all of their stakeholders. Corporate reporting should contribute to greater transparency and a clear and direct understanding of the company's past and current performance and future plans to avoid information asymmetry.

Every year, Benefit Corporations must communicate their economic and social results to stakeholders (Ferioli, 2022b) via a non-financial statement, which can be included in their financial statement. According to Italian Art. 1, para. 383, of Law no. 208 of December 28, 2015, this document must be made public on companies' websites. Thanks to the non-financial report, it is possible to make available to all stakeholders how much a company has invested in social and environmental issues and what actions they have undertaken in support of social inclusion and environmental respect. Communication of a Benefit Corporation's values must not be done for the sole purpose of improving the company's image; it must, instead, concretely involve all stakeholders. For this reason, the Italian Business Reporting Network (NIBR, 2019) did not rigidly define the parts to be included in the non-financial report. Instead, they ask organizations to value all present and future experiences that allow for the maximum expressiveness of this movement. The regulatory requirement regarding impact assessment is a challenge. The non-financial statement must include the following:

- A description of the objectives, actions, and methods for achieving the stated social benefits. If some social benefits are not achieved, justifications must be provided.
- A description of the social objectives that will be achieved in the following year.
- An evaluation of the company's activities in the following areas: corporate governance, employees, environment, and other interested parties.

Italian law adopted the B Impact Assessment (BIA) architecture developed by B Lab specifically for measuring the impact of Benefit

Corporations as a reference for the impact report (Shields & Shelleman, 2017).

Certified B Corps measure the quality and relevance of their impacts on society in a complete, transparent, and rigorous manner, which is shared annually with stakeholders through an impact report, using for this purpose the BIA (Benefit Impact Assessment) standard developed by B Lab. The impact assessment measures employed to evaluate sustainability performance must be provided by external assessment standards and developed by an independent and credible entity. These standards must be complete, articulated, and transparent. Any organization that receives the B-Corp Certification must agree for B Lab to make their B Impact Report, basic profile information, and any additional disclosures available, as required, on www.bcorporation.net and other B Lab affiliated websites (i.e., B Lab and Sistema B Global Partner websites). There are additional transparency requirements for certain wholly-owned or majority-owned subsidiaries and certain public companies.

Transparency as the basis of a B Corp's values translates into the commitment to evaluate and publicly report their results and impacts on society in a structured way that is constant over time (Cetindamar, 2018). The BIA allows organizations to evaluate their ability to create (or destroy) value by analyzing their business model, the quality of their relationships with their employees and stakeholders, and their responsibility for their environmental impacts.

In recent years, organizations are increasingly disclosing financial and non-financial information through integrated reporting thanks to the developing trend toward an integrated way of thinking. However, social communication is affected by the size of companies because this activity generates a cost that cannot be sustained by all companies equally. Larger companies are already subject to rigorous reporting standards. They are more likely to communicate social responsibility in a more complete and detailed way than smaller companies, which often do not have the resources to devote to this activity and prefer to focus their investments elsewhere. Therefore, social communication is often considered a residual activity for smaller companies. However, this is not true for Benefit Corporations and Certified B Corps because, despite their size, they have higher transparency standards than traditional companies. It is important to remember that social communication is a long-term investment that does not bring measurable results in the short term (Ferioli, 2022b; Ferioli et al., 2022).

The law and B Lab impose different transparency requirements between Benefit Corporations and Certified B Corps, respectively. The latter use the B Impact score, a quantitative measure, while the law does not impose specific measures on Benefit Corporations.

By communicating qualitative information, social performance is based on measures strongly influenced by subjective perceptions (Ferioli, 2022b; Ferioli et al., 2022). It makes it difficult to estimate the actual benefit generated and compare the impacts produced by different companies. For this reason, it is preferable to adopt quantitative measures that allow stakeholders to rely on objective assessments (Ferioli 2022b).

4.6 Disclosure on ESG and SDGs for Benefit Corporations and Certified B Corps and the Global Reporting Initiative

Companies are assessed on all five stakeholder groups and cannot choose to only be evaluated according to some groups. They have to answer an average of 200 questions, which can vary according to their size, sector and geography, and cover all the areas previously mentioned.

Benefit Corporations are an emerging economic phenomenon, but it is already clear that the main reporting document of business activities is more or less directly impacted by them. Sustainability reporting can only be achieved through accounting practices that embrace environmental, social, and governance (ESG) issues, which can effectively fuel a company's transition toward a sustainable and integrated approach. ESG is also valid at the corporate strategy level and in managing decision-making processes.

The problems associated with climate change and the COVID-19 pandemic led to an increase in the perception of the need to integrate sustainability issues, including environmental ones, into production processes, as well as to definitively move from a linear model to a circular economy model, which was also accepted and highlighted by the UN Agenda 2030.

In fact, Benefit Corporations are the result of a global movement aimed at spreading a more advanced and integrated business paradigm. Despite being "for profit," Benefit Corporations are oriented to achieve sustainable success for all stakeholders, including their employees, their community, and the environment.

Companies can choose which reporting models to refer to, opting, for example, for the use of the global reporting initiative (GRI) Standards, widely recognized as a point of reference for reporting on sustainability issues. Using the GRI Standards has some advantages. They are designed to promote global comparability, accessibility, and quality of information relating to the most significant economic, environmental, and social impacts. Therefore, a company's contributions to the goal of sustainable development favor greater transparency and accountability (Lingenfelter & Cohen, 2019).

GRI and B Lab joined forces to help organizations get more out of their reporting and assessment tools. This collaboration allows companies to optimize their contribution to a more sustainable future. The GRI Standards are the world's most widely adopted sustainability reporting standards, and the B Impact Assessment (BIA), from B Lab, is a tool to help organizations measure and manage their impact on all of their stakeholders. While fulfilling different purposes, GRI reporting and B Lab's BIA both help companies increase their awareness and transparency of their impacts. Putting information together allows organizations to manage and communicate it all together. B Lab and GRI (2021) published a document that provides an overview of how to use GRI Standards and B Lab's B Impact Assessment together and shows how they are complementary.

Moreover, in the future, it will become increasingly important for businesses to align their sustainability reporting with the SDGs (Mion, 2020). One of the crucial roles of sustainability reporting is to highlight the impact of an organization's activities on the 2030 Agenda, thus allowing for the progress of the implementation of the SDGs to be monitored. Companies can consider each SDG by looking at how it interacts with their business model, internal operations, supply chain, potential for collective action, and risk of negative impact. SDGs are the path to a sustainable future. Mapping the SDGs allows them to be easily identified and then integrated into the GRI standards so that an organization's contributions to these global objectives can be highlighted (Diez-Busto et al., 2021).

References

Bauer, J., & Umlas, E. (2017). Making corporations responsible: The parallel tracks of the B Corp movement and the business and human rights movement. *Business and Society Review*, *122*(3), 285–325. 10.1111/basr.12118

B Corporation (2022). Section "B Lab" – "About B Lab". Available at: https://bcorporation.eu/

B Corporation (2023). Make business a force for good. Available at: https://www.bcorporation.net/en-us/?_ga=2.240252035.1697298263.1674079923-593602033.1673861612

B Impact Assessment. (2021). B Corp Certification steps. Available at: https://kb.bimpactassessment.net/en/support/solutions/articles/43000015907-b-corp-certification-steps

B Impact Assessment. (2022). Here's how it works. Available at: https://www.bcorporation.net/en-us/programs-and-tools/b-impact-assessment

B Lab (2022). Available at: https://www.bcorporation.net/en-us/

B Lab Europe. (2021). Cosa sono le Società Benefit? Available at: https://www.societabenefit.net/cosa-sono-le-societa-benefit/

B Lab & GRI (2021). Complementary use and linkage of the GRI Standards and B Lab's B Impact Assessment. Available at: https://www.globalreporting.org/media/z53l0gdm/gri-b-lab-mapping-publication.pdf

Blasi, S., & Sedita, S.R. (2021). Mapping the emergence of a new organisational form: An exploration of the intellectual structure of the B Corp research. *Corporate Social Responsibility and Environmental Management, 29*(1) 107–123. 10.1002/csr.2187

Bocken, N.M.P., Rana, P., & Short, S.W. (2015). Value mapping for sustainable business thinking. *Journal of Industrial and Production Engineering, 32*(1), 67–81. 10.1080/21681015.2014.1000399

Burger-Helmchen, T., & Siegel, E.J. (2020). Some thoughts on CSR in relation to B Corp labels. *Entrepreneurship Research Journal, 10*(4), 1–19. 10.1515/erj-202 0-0231

Certificazione B Corporation (2021) Cambiare il mondo è possibile il primo report delle B Corp italiane. Available at: https://unlockthechange.it/app/uploads/2022/07/report.pdf

Cetindamar, D. (2018). Designed by law: Purpose, accountability, and transparency at benefit corporations. *Cogent Business & Management, 5*(1), 1423787. 10.1080/23311975.2018.1423787

Choi, T.M., Lo, C.K., Wong, C.W., & Yee, R.W. (2012). Green manufacturing and distribution in the fashion and apparel industries. *International Journal of Production Economics, 135*(2), 531. 10.1016/j.ijpe.2011.07.012

Diez-Busto, E., Sanchez-Ruiz, L., & Fernandez-Laviada, A. (2021). The B Corp movement: A systematic literature review. *Sustainability, 13*(5), 2508. 10.3390/su13052508

Ferioli, M. (2022a). B Corp: Un nuovo modello di business per la Mobilità Sostenibile. Il Caso del Gruppo Maganetti. *Economia Aziendale Online, 13*(1), 53–73. 10.13132/2038-5498/13.1.53-73

Ferioli, M. (2022b). Sustainability report as a non-financial disclosure tool for B-Corps: Analysis of the Italian fashion industry. *Economia Aziendale Online, 13*(3), 459–478. 10.13132/2038-5498/13.3.459-478

Ferioli, M., Freitas, M., & Spulber, D. (2021). The freedom to be sustainable, from the past to the future. *Geopolitical, Social Security and Freedom Journal, 4*(2), 59–79. 10.2478/gssfj-2021-0012

Ferioli, M., Gazzola, P., Grechi, D., & Vătămănescu, E.M. (2022). Sustainable behaviour of B Corps fashion companies during Covid-19: A quantitative economic analysis. *Journal of Cleaner Production, 374*, 134010. 10.1016/j.jclepro.2022.134010

Gazzola, P., Grechi, D., Ossola, P., & Pavione, E. (2019). Certified Benefit Corporations as a new way to make sustainable business: The Italian example. *Corporate Social Responsibility and Environmental Management, 26*(6), 1435–1445. 10.1002/csr.1758

Gazzola, P., Paterson, A., Amelio, S., & Ferioli, M. (2022). Certified B Corporations and innovation: Crowdfunding as a tool for Sustainability. *Sustainability, 14*(24), 16639. 10.3390/su142416639

Gazzola, P., Pavione, E., Grechi, D., & Raimondi, V. (2020). L'economia circolare nella fashion industry, ridurre, riciclare e riutilizzare: Alcuni esempi di successo. *Economia Aziendale Online, 11*(2), 165–174. 10.13132/2038-5498/11.2.165-174

Geerts, M., & Dooms, M. (2020). Sustainability reporting for inland port managing bodies: A stakeholder-based view on materiality. *Sustainability, 12*(5), 1726. 10.3390/su12051726

Honeyman, R., & Jana, T. (2019). *The B Corp handbook: How you can use business as a force for good.* Berrett-Koehler Publishers.

Joshi, Y., & Rahman, R. (2015). Factors affecting green purchase behaviour and future research directions. *International Strategic Management Review, 3*(1–2), 128–143. 10.1016/j.ism.2015.04.001

Khandker, S.R., Koolwal, G.B., & Samad, H.A. (2009). *Handbook on impact evaluation: Quantitative methods and practices.* World Bank Publications.

Kim, Y. (2021). Certified corporate social responsibility? The current state of certified and decertified B Corps. *Corporate Social Responsibility and Environmental Management, 28*(6), 1760–1768. 10.1002/csr.2147

Lee, J., & Lee, Y. (2018). Effects of multi-brand company's CSR activities on purchase intention through a mediating role of corporate image and brand image. *Journal of Fashion Marketing and Management: An International Journal, 22*(3), 387–403. 10.1108/JFMM-08-2017-0087

Lingenfelter, G., & Cohen, R. (2019). To B or not to B: Etsy's decision whether to re-incorporate as a public benefit corporation and maintain its B Lab certification. *The CASE Journal, 15*(6), 510–527. 10.1108/TCJ-06-2018-0069

Maccaferri, A. (2021). La pandemia spinge le BCorp: +26% in Italia nel 2021, Sole 24 ore, 21 febbraio 2022.

Mion, G. (2020). Organizations with impact? A study on Italian benefit corporations reporting practices and reporting quality. *Sustainability, 12*(21), 9038. 10.3390/su12219038

Mion, G., & Adaui, L.C.R. (2020). Understanding the purpose of benefit corporations: An empirical study on the Italian case. *International Journal of Corporate Social Responsibility, 5*(4), 1–15. 10.1186/s40991-020-00050-6

Mion, G., Adaui, L.C.R., & Bonfanti, A. (2021). Characterizing the mission statements of benefit corporations: Empirical evidence from Italy. *Business Strategy and the Environment, 30*(4), 2160–2172. 10.1002/bse.2738

Nativa. (2021). *The B book: Il grande libro delle B Corp italiane.* Nativa, 1–88.

Nave, A., & Ferreira, J. (2019). Corporate social responsibility strategies: Past research and future challenges. *Corporate Social Responsibility and Environmental Management, 26*(4), 885–901. 10.1002/csr.1729

NIBR – Network Italiano Business Reporting (2019). Linee Guida sul Reporting delle Società Benefit. Gruppo di Lavoro su "Il Reporting delle Società Benefit: principi, struttura e metriche." Available at: https://www.saracirone.com/wp-content/uploads/2019/04/NIBR_GUIDA-SB_ITA.pdf.

Nigri, G., Del Baldo, M., & Agulini, A. (2020). Governance and accountability models in Italian certified benefit corporations. *Corporate Social Responsibility and Environmental Management, 27*(5), 2368–2380. 10.1002/csr.1949

Nigri, G., Michelini, L., & Grieco, C. (2017). Social impact and online communication in B-Corps. *Global Journal of Business Research, 11*(3), 87–104. Available at: https://ssrn.com/abstract=3071156

Porter, M.E., & Kramer, M.R. (2019). Creating shared value. In *Managing sustainable business* (pp. 323–346). Springer.

Riolfo, G. (2020). The new Italian benefit corporation. *European Business Organization Law Review, 21*(2), 279–317. 10.1007/s40804-019-00149-9

Romolini, A., Fissi, S., & Gori, E. (2014). Scoring CSR reporting in listed companies—evidence from Italian best practices. *Corporate Social*

Responsibility and Environmental Management, *21*(2), 65–81. 10.1002/csr.1299

Shields, J.F., & Shelleman, J.M. (2017). A method to launch sustainability reporting in SMEs: The B Corp impact assessment framework. *Journal of Strategic Innovation & Sustainability*, *12*(2), 10–19. 10.33423/jsis.v12i2.798

Stammer, R. (2016). It pays to become a B corporation. *Harvard Business Review*, December 6, 2016.

Stubbs, W. (2017). Characterising B Corps as a sustainable business model: An exploratory study of B Corps in Australia. *Journal of Cleaner Production*, *144*, 299–312. 10.1016/j.jclepro.2016.12.093

Villela, M., Bulgacov, S., & Morgan, G. (2021). B Corp certification and its impact on organizations over time. *Journal of Business Ethics*, *170*, 343–357. 10.1007/s10551-019-04372-9

Vu, T., Nguyen, N., Nguyen, X., Nguyen, Q., & Nguyen, H. (2020). Corporate social responsibility, employee commitment, reputation, government support and financial performance in Vietnam's export textile enterprises. *Accounting*, *6*(6), 1045–1058. 10.5267/j.ac.2020.7.015

Wray, V. (2015). Communicating social impact. Retrieved June 25, 2016, from https://www.conference-board.org/publications/publicationdetail.cfm?publicationid=2968&centerId=1

5 The Italian fashion industry: B Corps case study

5.1 The fast fashion industry and the challenges of sustainability

Currently worth over three trillion US dollars, the fashion industry is one of the largest and fastest-growing industries in the world. Thus, it plays a key role in achieving the UN's 2030 Agenda for Sustainable Development. It aligns with other creative industries, such as product design and architecture, because the goods produced are characterized by creativity, and functionality is not their main feature. This means that consumers buy fashion products for their symbolic characteristics, using clothes, fabrics, styles, etc., to personalize their image as a status symbol or to display a social position or a particular lifestyle (Thorisdottir & Johannsdottir, 2020). Fashion is a mature industry, characterized by short life cycles, intense competition, high volatility in demand, high impulse buying, high-cost pressure, and low predictability (Čiarnienė & Vienažindienė, 2014; Adam et al., 2018). For this reason, it often relies on a low-cost structure that exploits low-cost production methods and a low-price policy (Thorisdottir & Johannsdottir, 2020).

Fast fashion and mass production have led to a level of consumerism that has created a culture of waste and an increase in environmental pollution (Thorisdottir & Johannsdottir, 2020). Fast fashion has changed the shopping experience by enabling consumers to obtain an abundance of items at affordable prices. Moreover, consumers are increasingly demanding shorter delivery times, increasing the need to produce faster (Čiarnienė & Vienažindienė, 2014). In addition, the wide availability of size and color combinations has resulted in high volumes of orders delivered to stores every two weeks (Čiarnienė & Vienažindienė, 2014; Thorisdottir & Johannsdottir, 2020). To follow this strategy, some companies fail to prioritize safeguarding the well-being of their employees as well as the planet. Indeed, the industry has repeatedly been accused of using marketing strategies to promote the kind of consumerism that leads to sustainability challenges because non-renewable resources are used to produce these new clothes that are thrown away when they become

DOI: 10.4324/9781003388470-6

unfashionable (Ellen MacArthur Foundation, 2017; Thorisdottir & Johannsdottir, 2020; Provin & de Aguiar Dutra, 2021). This often happens before consumers have even worn the clothes (Ellen MacArthur Foundation, 2017; Thorisdottir & Johannsdottir, 2020). Most waste products are lost to landfills or incinerated (Ellen MacArthur Foundation, 2017), resulting in a strong negative impact on the natural environment and society (Ellen MacArthur Foundation, 2017).

Buying clothing that respects the environment and people can cost double or even more than the items sold by fast fashion chains that attract customers with low prices. In other words, an ethical and sustainable lifestyle can represent higher costs for the consumer. However, we must not forget that environmental and social costs are hidden behind a low price. Unsustainable practices also generate negative effects on the global economy (Gazzola et al., 2020b; Thorisdottir & Johannsdottir, 2020). Therefore, a new approach to waste management is needed (Provin & de Aguiar Dutra, 2021).

One indicator that supports sustainable purchasing is to calculate the cost per wear (CPW). The cost per wear indicates the result obtained by dividing the cost of a garment by the number of times it is worn. In this way, it becomes easier to highlight how paying a low cost for a dress or accessory that will almost never be worn is both environmentally and economically harmful. The more the garment is worn, the more its cost is amortized (Goldsworthy, 2017). Buying a quality garment lowers the cost per wear because the product lasts longer over time and can be used more. Garments made from natural fibers, for example, are more resistant than those made with synthetic fibers and also tend to be damaged less by the washing process.

5.2 The impacts of the fashion industry

The concept of sustainable fashion is fashion that is attentive to the needs of society and the environment. The guiding principles of sustainable fashion range from the recycling and reuse of clothes to the choice of ecological and natural fabrics, all united by technological innovation, which can generate production models that attend even more to the needs of the planet. The new business model includes recycling, reselling, renting, reusing, and repairing (Pucker, 2022).

Sustainable fashion dates to the 18th century, when men's vests were reused to make new women's vests (Thorisdottir & Johannsdottir, 2020). The need for social responsibility in the industry emerged as early as the 1990s' supply chain revolution (Caniato et al., 2012). However, the fashion industry has been slow to implement sustainable actions, and only a few companies have hired corporate social responsibility (CSR) experts to address sustainability issues (Thorisdottir & Johannsdottir,

2020). Over the years, the industry has been blamed for its negative ecological footprint (Chan et al., 2020; Thorisdottir & Johannsdottir, 2020). In fact, together with textiles, it is the most polluting and resource-intensive industry (Provin et al., 2021). The unsustainable activities are mainly associated with the production processes which involve the intense use of energy, chemical products, natural resources, and labor abuses (Caniato et al., 2012; Provin & de Aguiar Dutra, 2021). Moreover, the production and distribution of traditional fashion and clothing products are known to generate high volumes of waste and scrap, releasing pollutants such as dye chemicals and toxic gases (Choi et al., 2012). The industry also employs energy-inefficient production and distribution methods (Choi et al., 2012). Research conducted by the Ellen MacArthur Foundation (2017) found that 500 billion US dollars are lost every year due to non-recycled and discarded clothing (Ellen MacArthur Foundation, 2017; Gazzola et al., 2020b). Furthermore, it is estimated that more than half of fast-fashion products are disposed of in under a year (Ellen MacArthur Foundation, 2017). Specifically, every second, the equivalent amount of a garbage truck of textiles is burned or taken to a landfill (Ellen MacArthur Foundation, 2017; Gazzola et al., 2020b). According to the Ellen Macarthur Foundation (2017), the main reasons why people throw away clothes are the following: didn't fit anymore (42%); didn't like anymore (26%); the dress is damaged, stained, lost shape, or worn out (19%); and didn't need anymore (7%).

The fashion industry uses over 98 million tons of non-renewable resources per year, including fertilizers for cotton farms, petroleum to produce synthetic fibers, and chemicals to produce and dye fabrics (Ellen MacArthur Foundation, 2017; Gazzola et al., 2020b). The production processes involve 93 billion cubic meters of water, which, in addition to worsening droughts, releases the equivalent of over 50 billion plastic bottles into the ocean (Ellen MacArthur Foundation, 2017; Gazzola et al., 2020b). These processes contribute to emissions of 1.2 billion tons of CO_2 (Ellen MacArthur Foundation, 2017; Gazzola et al., 2020b). The most used natural fiber in the clothing industry is cotton (Hansen & Schaltegger, 2013). Its production accounts for 7% of employment in developing countries and plays an important role in worsening environmental pollution (Hansen & Schaltegger, 2013; Ellen MacArthur Foundation, 2017; Gazzola et al., 2020b). Indeed, cotton is grown in monocultures that use very high amounts of pesticides and chemical fertilizers that reduce biodiversity in the long run. Furthermore, it is responsible for the displacement of the local population and the decrease of virgin forests (Hansen & Schaltegger, 2013). Finally, production is often carried out in underdeveloped and labor-intensive countries, where the manufacturing processes often involve child labor, low incomes, and slave labor conditions (Ellen MacArthur Foundation, 2017; Chan et al.,

2020; Gazzola et al., 2020b). In this way, the fashion industry contributes to the presence of sweatshops, where workplaces are unsafe, wages are low, and workers' rights are violated (Thorisdottir & Johannsdottir, 2020; Provin & de Aguiar Dutra, 2021).

Over the years, these problems have prevented sustainable development in developing countries (Thorisdottir & Johannsdottir, 2020). After the collapse of the Rana Plaza building in Bangladesh in 2013, attention to workers' rights and decent working conditions increased (Il Sole 24 Ore, 2013; Thorisdottir & Johannsdottir, 2020). However, social responsibility actions must be taken soon to prevent the industry from generating the equivalent of a quarter of global carbon emissions by 2050 (Gazzola et al., 2020b). Immediate actions could produce 192 billion US dollars in social and environmental benefits by 2030 (Ellen MacArthur Foundation, 2017).

Sustainability has become a popular topic in all sectors during the last decade (Choi et al., 2012; Gazzola et al., 2020b). As previously described, CSR requires companies to address economic, social, and environmental issues (Gazzola, 2012b; Battistini & Gazzola, 2015; Ferioli et al., 2021). Companies are held accountable for both their unsustainable behaviors and the environmental performance of their suppliers and partners.

Consumers are increasingly asking companies to be transparent regarding its sustainable practices, and this leads to the domino effect: if a company is sustainable, its suppliers must be too. Therefore, it is necessary to trace the entire route that a garment has taken before reaching the final consumer. Moreover, greater information sharing is possible today thanks to technologies such as the blockchain, a method still little adopted by companies, but which is also able to give guarantees against counterfeiting (Caldarelli et al., 2021). Ultimately, sustainability must be considered in the whole value chain (Caniato et al., 2012; Čiarnienė & Vienažindienė, 2014; Gazzola et al., 2020a), and this means that fashion companies must rely on partners who engage in socially responsible behaviors (Caniato et al., 2012). To make the industry sustainable, fashion companies should approach sustainability as an opportunity for the future and a long-term vision for protecting our economic, social, and natural resources (Thorisdottir & Johannsdottir, 2020).

In the past, consumers have not shown much interest in purchasing eco-friendly products because the design did not appeal to them (Thorisdottir & Johannsdottir, 2020). De Angelis et al. (2017) explained that this type of product was not marketed the way other high fashion products were; therefore, consumers perceived them differently. To overcome this problem, designers should provide more value to eco-friendly clothing models without damaging the brand identity or style (De Angelis et al., 2017). Recently, consumers have become more interested in buying sustainable products (Choi et al., 2012; Gazzola et al., 2020b). Gazzola et al. (2020a) demonstrated that 90% of young people are increasingly demanding sustainable fashion (Gazzola et al., 2020b, 2020c). Specifically, 41% of those belonging to Generation Z (people born between 1997 and 2012) and 28% of Millennials (people born between 1981 and 1996) prioritize personal and planetary health in their purchasing decisions (Gazzola et al., 2020b). Furthermore, 28% of Generation Z and 22% of Millennials look for sustainable brand products (Gazzola et al., 2020b) and are willing to pay premium prices for eco-fashion (Choi et al., 2012; Gazzola et al., 2020b).

5.3 The need of green business practices

Consumers' increased attention to social and environmental sustainability created the need for companies to adopt greener business practices (Caniato et al., 2012; Gazzola et al., 2020a, 2020b). Compared to the past, fashion companies are more committed to social responsibility activities than ever before (Caniato et al., 2012; Gazzola et al., 2020b). Many of them are adopting standards and codes of conduct to manage the impacts that their supply chain has on society and the environment (Pedersen et al., 2018). Some companies have also joined the green fashion movement and the fashion pact,[1] which is a coalition of 200 global fashion brands committed to halting global warming, restoring biodiversity, and protecting the oceans (Gazzola et al., 2020b). In the last two years, the number of events dedicated to sustainability in the fashion sector has increased. For example, Rome (Italy) hosted three events[2:]

1 *September 2020—Sustainable Innovation Fashion Week*: The first event in Italy dedicated to innovation in green fashion. More than 120 brands participated in the event, and each of them presented a vision of the future that combines advanced technologies and innovative materials.
2 *May 2021—Phygital Sustainability EXPO*: The first event in Italy dedicated to the eco-sustainable transition of fashion and design. It represents one of the first events in the world dedicated to the ecological transition of the fashion sector. The event promoted awareness for the consumption of fashion garments compliant with the 2030 SDGs.
3 *July 2021—Green Confidential for Startups Awards*: Call for startups: "seeking the unicorn firm in fashion tech": It was the first edition of an annual award given to startups in the sustainability and fashion tech sector with high technological and innovative content. The thematic areas concern fashion tech (i.e., digital technologies applied to fashion), accessible fashion (i.e., wearable devices, inclusive garments,

and integrated projects), and smart fabrics (i.e., technical fabrics and circular fabrics). The prize is conferred to business projects that contribute to the achievement of the United Nations' SDGs by introducing sustainable practices in the fashion sector.

However, the fashion industry still needs a comprehensive plan to address sustainability, including policies to create long-term value and innovation in business models (Montanino et al., 2020). To this end, companies should pursue the United Nations' Sustainable Development Goals (SDGs) because they are a tool to encourage sustainable strategies and meet societal expectations (Clarke-Sather & Cobb K., 2019).

In 2022, the European Commission proposed a series of objectives aimed at supporting the fashion sector in transitioning to a sustainable model (Buchel et al., 2022). The objectives are as follows:

- Ban articles produced without respect for fundamental human rights from the European market.
- Ban greenwashing by asking companies to support their sustainability communications with sound scientific evidence.
- Only export used clothes to countries that demonstrate the will and ability to manage it.
- Favor the choice of non-synthetic materials by blocking the use of microplastics.
- Increase transparency regarding the final consumer by informing them of the origin of all clothing components.
- Limit the number of collections per year.
- Make it illegal to destroy unsold clothing.
- Manage the end of life of each item produced; companies will pay a dedicated tax, which will serve to enhance collection, recovery, and recycling systems.
- Research and innovate to develop new technologies for the recycling of textile materials and new bio-based materials.

In January 2023, the European Commission launched the "ReSet the Trend" campaign aimed at educating consumers about sustainability and fighting fast fashion, which is believed to be a major cause of pollution (European Union, 2023). Since January 1, 2022, the obligation to separate collection of textile products has been in force in Italy, and by 2023 it will be illegal to destroy unsold goods in France, thanks to a revolutionary "anti-waste" law. The commission raises stakeholders' awareness of the benefits associated with transforming the textile sector and the opportunities that sustainable fashion offers both to businesses and consumers (Eppinger, 2022).

5.4 The Italian fashion industry

The Italian fashion industry is developed in districts, and it accounts for 12.5% of employment in the manufacturing industry, with 8.5% turnover (exceeding 80 billion euros). Moreover, it employs 500,000 people, 310,000 of whom are employed in micro-small businesses (Montanino et al., 2020). Although it has lower productivity on average than the manufacturing industry due to the demand for increasingly quality products (which characterize the Made in Italy branding), it has grown more rapidly since 2007 with an average annual growth rate of 1.3%. Italian fashion companies are, on average, micro, small, and medium enterprises, and their dimension is lower than the European Union average. Precisely, more than 60% of the textile, clothing, leather, accessories, and fashion industry enterprises are small and micro-businesses. The small size allows companies to be more flexible, have a high degree of specialization, innovate more, and compete in international markets. The ability to compete is confirmed by the industry's export performance and by the important role they play in the European market, evidenced as follows (Montanino et al., 2020):

- 33.3% of the value generated by the European Union's fashion industry is associated with Italy.
- 60% of fashion in the world comes from Italian companies.
- 70% of Italian fashion exports are high-end.
- 77.8% of EU exports are from the Italian textile industry. Medium-large international brands rely on Italian companies for their supplies.

According to Kearney's Circular Fashion Index 2022, Italy is the second most sustainable country in terms of fashion production, following France. Italian fashion is based on a long tradition of craftsmanship, and it's famous for the quality of the fabrics. Today, however, it is not enough to have a high-quality product. Made in Italy must manage the transition toward sustainability. The entire Italian fashion industry is now moving toward increasingly ethical and green production. Precisely because it represents leadership in the industry, it can lead this change. Sustainability has also become a fundamental competitive lever to meet the approval of increasingly attentive stakeholders. More and more consumers want to make a difference and are committed to fighting fast fashion through the creation of various start-ups, with the aim of making stakeholders aware of the issue of sustainability. Many start-ups designed to help consumers become more and more green have been born in Italy (Ciccullo et al., 2023).

Fashion will increasingly have to follow an approach based on reducing the use of resources by reusing, recycling, and optimizing the use of raw materials—a change that can be facilitated by technology and the drive for innovation, but which, in order to be truly effective, will necessarily have to train a new generation of entrepreneurs to develop processes, products, and business models based on sustainability and social responsibility. The European Commission is pushing for the creation of recycling hubs, at the European and national levels, to manage the recycling of processing waste (pre- and post-consumer) and waste from the separate collection of textiles. The Italian city of Prato, one of the largest industrial districts in Italy, the largest textile center in Europe, and one of the most important poles in the world for the production of wool yarns and fabrics, is also a pioneer of Italian textile recycling and has already set up the first textile hub (Caliskan, 2022).

5.5 B Corps in the Italian fashion industry

Companies in the Italian fashion industry are increasingly adopting innovative business models that allow them to be profitable while also facing the challenges posed by sustainability. Among the 200 Italian B Corps (as of January 31, 2022), 11 fashion companies have adopted the Certified B Corps innovative business model; of these, 81.82% are also B Corps (Figure 5.1).

As discussed in the previous chapter, B Corps are defined as hybrid organizations because their activities make it possible to merge economic, social, and environmental objectives (Mion & Loza Adaui, 2020; Riolfo, 2020; Ferioli, 2022a). Their business model can be an effective way to make the fashion industry more sustainable. For this reason, their activities are in line with sustainable development and the United Nations' SDGs.

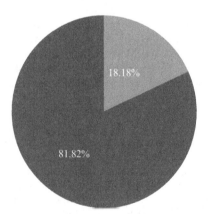

■ Certified B Corps   ■ Certified B Corps who are also Benefit Corporations

Figure 5.1 Italian fashion Certified B Corps and B Corps.

As we have seen, social communication is a crucial aspect of B Corps, as they are subject to higher accountability, transparency, and purpose standards. It allows them to establish positive relationships with stakeholders because they are interested in knowing how companies contribute to the environment and the well-being of society (Romolini et al., 2014; Joshi & Rahman, 2015; Lee & Lee, 2018; Nave & Ferreira, 2019). Furthermore, social communication facilitates corporate legitimacy and mitigates legislative pressures (Gazzola, 2012a; Romolini et al., 2014; Gazzola et al., 2020a; Ferioli et al., 2021). All B Corps belonging to the Italian fashion industry communicate their social responsibility as an attachment to their financial statements, on their website home page, and on a webpage dedicated to tracking their impacts on society and the environment. In line with the requirements imposed by Italian law, the leading document used to report these impacts is the sustainability report (non-financial statement); 63.64% make this document available through their websites (Figure 5.2).

This aspect should be improved in the future to fulfill their obligations and allow stakeholders to exhaustively evaluate the companies' CSR. In fact, as we saw in the third chapter, the sustainability report is a fundamental tool for pursuing internal and external analyses (Brogonzoli, 2005).

The SDGs represent a guide for companies to achieve sustainable development by 2030. The result of the analysis shows that 72.73% of B Corps explicitly communicate whether or not they pursue the SDGs through their sustainability report and website, indicating which aspects of sustainable development management they are focusing on (Figure 5.3).

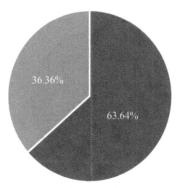

- B Corps who publish the sustainability report on their website
- B Corps who do not make the sustainability report available on their website

Figure 5.2 B Corps who publish their sustainability report on their websites.

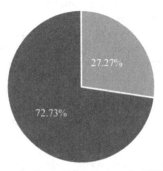

    ■ B Corps who do not claim to pursue the UN SDGs
    ■ B Corps explicitly stating that they pursue the UN SDGs

Figure 5.3 B Corps claiming to pursue the United Nations Sustainable
    Development Goals (UN SDGs).

Specifically, all companies that publish a sustainability report communicate the SDGs they are pursuing in it, while 40% of those who do
not make this document available, declare their pursuance of SDGs
through their websites (Figure 5.4).

The SDGs most pursued by the Italian fashion B Corps are numbers
8 ("Decent working and economic growth") and 12 ("Responsible
consumption and production"). In second place, we find SDGs 9
("Industry, innovation, and infrastructure") and 13 ("Climate action").
On the other hand, the SDGs not pursued by any Italian fashion B

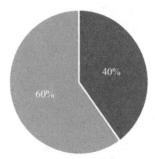

    ■ B Corps who claim to pursue the SDGs only on the website.
    ■ B Corps not pursuing SDGs.

Figure 5.4 Certified B Corps claiming to pursue the United Nations Sustainable
    Development Goals (SDGs).

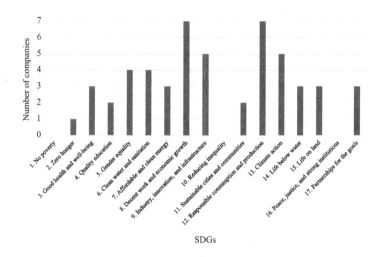

Figure 5.5 The most pursued Sustainable Development Goals (SDGs) by Italian fashion B Corps.

Corps are numbers 1 ("No poverty"), 10 ("Reduced inequalities"), and 16 ("Peace, justice, and strong institutions") (Figure 5.5).

Approximately 9% of B Corps in the fashion industry also publish other sustainability documents (Figure 5.6).

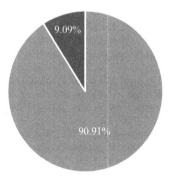

- B Corps that do not publish other sustainability documents
- B Corps that also publish other sustainability documents

Figure 5.6 The most pursued Sustainable Development Goals by Italian fashion B Corps.

These documents provide accurate information to stakeholders, as they report specific aspects of sustainability, such as raw materials, production techniques, and internal processes.

Finally, despite the growing trend toward integrated reporting and integrated thinking, the B Corps in the Italian fashion industry prefer to publish their sustainability reports separately from their financial ones. As we have seen, the integrated report allows stakeholders to appreciate the value they have generated and think of it as shared between society and the environment. Fashion B Corps should communicate more through this type of report because it shows how the company accessed and used different financial, human, and social resources using short-, medium-, and long-term perspectives (IIRC, 2011). However, social communication has a cost that is reflected in different ways according to the size of a company, the resources they possess, and the complexity of the report (Ferioli, 2022b). In addition, smaller and non-public companies may decide not to disclose their financial information to all stakeholders. Since Italian fashion companies are mainly small and medium-sized enterprises SMEs, the use of the integrated report is limited.

Notes

1 Source: https://thefashionpact.org/?lang=it
2 Source: https://www.sustainablefashioninnovation.org

References

Adam, M., Strähle, J., & Freise, M. (2018). Dynamic capabilities of early-stage firms: Exploring the business of renting fashion. *Journal of Small Business Strategy*, *28*(2), 49–67.

Battistini, C., & Gazzola, P. (2015). Is CSR just a matter of resources? *Economia Aziendale Online*, *6*(2), 43–47. 10.6092/2038-5498/6.2.43-47

Brogonzoli, L. (2005). *La rendicontazione sociale*. Elemond Scuola & Azienda, 6–17.

Buchel, S., Hebinck, A., Lavanga, M., & Loorbach, D. (2022). Disrupting the status quo: A sustainability transitions analysis of the fashion system. *Sustainability: Science, Practice and Policy*, *18*(1), 231–246. 10.1080/15487733. 2022.2040231

Caldarelli, G., Zardini, A., & Rossignoli, C. (2021). Blockchain adoption in the fashion sustainable supply chain: Pragmatically addressing barriers. *Journal of Organizational Change Management*, *34*(2), 507–524. 10.1108/JOCM-09-2020-0299

Caliskan, A. (2022). Seaports participation in enhancing the sustainable development goals. *Journal of Cleaner Production*, *379*, 134715. 10.1016/j.jclepro.2 022.134715

Caniato, F., Caridi, M., Crippa, L., & Moretto, A. (2012). Environmental sustainability in fashion supply chains: An exploratory case based research.

International Journal of Production Economics, *135*(2), 659–670. 10.1016/j.ijpe.2
011.06.001

Chan, H.L., Wei, X., Guo, S., & Leung, W.H. (2020). Corporate social responsibility (CSR) in fashion supply chains: A multi-methodological study.
Transportation Research Part E: Logistics and Transportation Review, *142*,
102063. 10.1016/j.tre.2020.102063

Choi, T.M., Lo, C.K., Wong, C.W., & Yee, R.W. (2012). Green manufacturing
and distribution in the fashion and apparel industries. *International Journal of
Production Economics*, *135*(2), 531. 10.1016/j.ijpe.2011.07.012

Čiarnienė, R., & Vienažindienė, M. (2014). Management of contemporary fashion
industry: Characteristics and challenges. *Procedia-Social and Behavioral
Sciences*, *156*, 63–68. 10.1016/j.sbspro.2014.11.120

Ciccullo, F., Pero, M., & Patrucco, A.S. (2023). Designing circular supply chains
in start-up companies: Evidence from Italian fashion and construction start-
ups. *The International Journal of Logistics Management*, *43*(3). 10.1108/IJLM-
04-2022-0158

Clarke-Sather, Abigail, & Cobb, Kelly (2019). Onshoring fashion: Worker sustainability impacts of global and local apparel production. *Journal of Cleaner
Production*, 208, 1206–1218. 10.1016/j.jclepro.2018.09.073

De Angelis, M., Adıgüzel, F., & Amatulli, C. (2017). The role of design similarity
in consumers' evaluation of new green products: An investigation of luxury
fashion brands. *Journal of Cleaner Production*, *141*, 1515–1527. 10.1016/
j.jclepro.2016.09.230

Ellen MacArthur Foundation. (2017). A new textiles economy: Redesigning
fashion's future. *Ellen MacArthur Foundation*, 3–117. Available at: https://
ellenmacarthurfoundation.org/a-new-textiles-economy

Eppinger, E. (2022). Recycling technologies for enabling sustainability transitions
of the fashion industry: Status quo and avenues for increasing post-consumer
waste recycling. *Sustainability: Science, Practice and Policy*, *18*(1), 114–128.
10.1080/15487733.2022.2027122

European Union. (2023). ReSet the Trend. Available at: https://environment.ec.
europa.eu/topics/circular-economy/reset-trend_en

Ferioli, M. (2022a). B Corp: Un Nuovo Modello di Business per la Mobilità
Sostenibile. Il Caso del Gruppo Maganetti. *Economia Aziendale Online*, *13*(1),
53–73. 10.13132/2038-5498/13.1.53-73

Ferioli, M. (2022b). Sustainability report as a non-financial disclosure tool for B-
Corps: Analysis of the Italian fashion industry. *Economia Aziendale Online*,
13(3), 459–478. 10.13132/2038-5498/13.3.459-478

Ferioli, M., Freitas, M., & Spulber, D. (2021). The freedom to be sustainable,
from the past to the future. *Geopolitical, Social Security and Freedom Journal*,
4(2), 59–79. 10.2478/gssfj-2021-0012

Gazzola, P. (2012a). La comunicazione sociale nella creazione di valore sostenibile. *Economia Aziendale Online*, (2), 11–24. 10.13132/2038-5498/2005.2.11-24

Gazzola, P. (2012b). *CSR per scelta o per necessità?* Santarcangelo di Romagna:
Maggioli, 13–138.

Gazzola, P., Pavione, E., & Dall'Ava, M. (2020a). I differenti significati
di sostenibilità per le aziende del lusso e della moda: Case studies a

confronto. *Economia Aziendale Online, 10*(4), 663–676. 10.13132/2038-54
98/10.4.2005

Gazzola, P., Pavione, E., Grechi, D., & Raimondi, V. (2020b). L'economia
circolare nella fashion industry, ridurre, riciclare e riutilizzare: Alcuni esempi
di successo. *Economia Aziendale Online, 11*(2), 165–174. 10.13132/2038-
5498/11.2.165-174

Gazzola, P., Pavione, E., Pezzetti, R., & Grechi, D. (2020c). Trends in the fashion
industry. The perception of sustainability and circular economy: A gender/
generation quantitative approach. *Sustainability, 12*(7), 2809. 10.3390/su12
072809

Goldsworthy, K. (2017). The speedcycle: A design-led framework for fast and
slow circular fashion lifecycles. *The Design Journal, 20*(sup1), S1960–S1970.
10.1080/14606925.2017.1352714

Hansen, E.G., & Schaltegger, S. (2013). 100 per cent organic? A sustainable entrepreneurship perspective on the diffusion of organic clothing. *Corporate
Governance, 13*(5), 583–598. 10.1108/CG-06-2013-0074

Il Sole 24 Ore. (2013). Bangladesh, estratta viva dopo 17 giorni dalle macerie del
Rana Plaza. I morti superano i mille. 10 maggio 2013. Available online: https://
st.ilsole24ore.com/art/notizie/2013-05-10/bangladesh-sono-mille-corpi-110229.
shtml?uuid=Abw8eduH

International Integrated Reporting Committee (IIRC). (2011). Towards integrated reporting—communicating value in the 21st century. *International
Integrated Reporting Committee Publications*, 3–4. Available at: www.
theiirc.org

Joshi, Y., & Rahman, Z. (2015). Factors affecting green purchase behaviour and
future research directions. *International Strategic Management Review, 3*(1–2),
128–143. 10.1016/j.ism.2015.04.001

Lee, J., & Lee, Y. (2018). Effects of multi-brand company's CSR activities on
purchase intention through a mediating role of corporate image and brand
image. *Journal of Fashion Marketing and Management: An International
Journal, 22*(3), 387–403. 10.1108/JFMM-08-2017-0087

Montanino, A., Iacovone, D., Daviddi, M., Ferri, D., Radoccia, S., &
Boccardelli, P. (2020). Settore Moda e Covid-19: Scenario, impatti, prospettive.
Cassa Depositi e Prestiti, Ernst & Young, Luiss Business School, 5–35.

Nave, A., & Ferreira, J. (2019). Corporate social responsibility strategies: Past
research and future challenges. *Corporate Social Responsibility and
Environmental Management, 26*(4), 885–901. 10.1002/csr.1729

Pedersen, E.R.G., Gwozdz, W., & Hvass, K.K. (2018). Exploring the relationship
between business model innovation, corporate sustainability, and organisational values within the fashion industry. *Journal of Business Ethics, 149*(2),
267–284. 10.1007/s10551-016-3044-7

Provin, A.P., & de Aguiar Dutra, A.R. (2021). Circular economy for fashion industry:
Use of waste from the food industry for the production of biotextiles. *Technological
Forecasting and Social Change, 169*, 120858. 10.1016/j.techfore.2021.120858

Provin, A.P., de Aguiar Dutra, A.R., Machado, M.M., & Cubas, A.L.V. (2021).
New materials for clothing: Rethinking possibilities through a sustainability
approach: A review. *Journal of Cleaner Production, 282*, 124444. 10.1016/
j.jclepro.2020.124444

Pucker, K.P. (2022). The myth of sustainable fashion. *Harvard Business Review*, *13*. https://hbr.org/2022/01/the-myth-of-sustainable-fashion

Riolfo, G. (2020). The new Italian benefit corporation. *European Business Organization Law Review*, *21*(2), 279–317. 10.1007/s40804-019-00149-9

Romolini, A., Fissi, S., & Gori, E. (2014). Scoring CSR reporting in listed companies—evidence from Italian best practices. *Corporate Social Responsibility and Environmental Management*, *21*(2), 65–81. 10.1002/csr.1299

Sustainable Fashion Innovation Society. Available online: https://www.sustainablefashioninnovation.org

The Fashion Pact. About the fashion pact. Available online: https://www.thefashionpact.org/?lang=it

Thorisdottir, T.S., & Johannsdottir, L. (2020). Corporate social responsibility influencing sustainability within the fashion industry. A systematic review. *Sustainability*, *12*(21), 9167 10.3390/su12219167

Conclusion

Corporate social responsibility has become the new imperative for long-term business success, as stakeholders have become increasingly interested in organizations' sustainable activities. The global business environment requires organizations to find ways to stay competitive and overcome threats through sustainable governance. A strong sustainable governance structure ensures that organizations develop a resilient capacity that allows them to react to unforeseen events, as the social and environmental impacts of organizations' activities jeopardize their profitability and their ability to survive in the long term. Thus, CSR helps ease financial constraints and facilitates market access.

In the context of sustainable development, organizations are evaluated along the dimensions of the triple bottom line (i.e., financial, environmental, and social sustainability). Stakeholders want to know about financial and non-financial performance, such as sustainability performance. An organization's ability to engage with stakeholders and integrate stakeholder knowledge promotes two-way communication, transparency, and appropriate feedback. This allows organizations to effectively disseminate information to stakeholders who are connected in a network of influences. In this way, they can respond to social and environmental pressures, gain insights to create growth opportunities, and drive the development of new markets. To this end, non-financial reporting is a useful reporting tool to achieve sustainable development in line with the European Union directive and the United Nations Sustainable Development Goals (SDGs). During the preparation of their non-financial declaration, companies carry out internal analyses that help them to identify corrective actions for the achievement of sustainable environmental, social, and governance performances. Furthermore, organizations are encouraged to include and define actions through which they intend to achieve the SDGs. For example, the action of implementing structured reporting related to the 2030 Agenda is a fundamental element for a transparent organization. In fact, social

DOI: 10.4324/9781003388470-7

reporting requires attempts to implement procedures that lead to non-financial reports that collect performance assessments and strategies related to the SDGs. Non-financial reporting should integrate the SDGs and combine them with environmental, social, and governance (ESG) metrics so that the organization has data and information on which to base their strategy, implement sustainable policies, and maintain an active dialogue with stakeholders. Furthermore, the adoption of a standard improves the comparability and transparency of effective information, enabling organizations to improve decision-making and actions toward the achievement of significant and measurable global objectives.

The international economic situation has increasingly led to reflections on the importance of continuous sustainable growth, mainly based on the 2030 SDGs, which include the fight against poverty and respect for human rights, labor and the environment. The sustainable transition asks companies to inform stakeholders on environmental, social, and governance sustainability. It is in this constantly evolving context of a sustainable approach to business models that the Benefit Corporation and B Corp movement was born. Benefit Corporations and Certified B Corps are complementary models. On the one hand, Benefit Corporations declare and share their mission, which they maintain in the medium and long term. Moreover, the company's corporate purpose is integrated with a description of the impacts on society and the environment that the company plans to pursue. The B Corp certification can be obtained only after passing the B Impact Assessment (BIA) with a minimum score verified by B Lab. As an emerging economic phenomenon, B Corps recognize the need for social responsibility without neglecting financial performance. B Corps adopt reporting documents that address ESG issues. In this way, they ensure that the company's strategy and decision-making processes follow an integrated and sustainable approach.

Climate change and the COVID-19 pandemic have increased the perception of the need to take immediate action toward a more sustainable future. The B Corps in the Italian fashion industry have adopted strategies and production processes that allow for their definitive transition from a linear model to a circular economy model in line with the 2030 Agenda of the United Nations. These B Corps are the result of a global movement to achieve sustainable success for all. They fulfill social communication needs by disclosing documents that provide accurate ESG information to stakeholders and also report specific aspects of sustainability. The Benefit Corporations and Certified B Corps in Italy have given life to a real movement aimed at accelerating the transition toward the creation of shared value. The Italian benefit movement is currently the fastest growing in Europe.

The fashion sector is one of the major polluters and producers of greenhouse gases in the world, mainly due to the consumption model of fast fashion, in which clothing is perceived to be a perishable good to be thrown away after a short use. The future of fashion companies depends a lot on sustainability. These are the new rules of the global market, where growing sensitivity toward environmental and social issues determines the need to combine profit with ethics. To ensure that at least one aspect of the product is sustainable, both companies and consumers rely, for example, on certifications that guarantee the origin of the yarns, recycling, or—even better—the analysis of the entire life cycle of a garment or yarn. Unlike these small and specific certifications, however, the B Corp certification is based on the whole company.

Today, companies, especially fashion companies, are asked not only to act responsibly, but also to communicate transparently. Sustainability must be fully integrated into the organization's strategy, culture, and entire value chain. This need derives from stakeholders' greater awareness of sustainability. In fact, a strong acceleration of the process toward sustainability is underway through the adoption of rules and regulations based on social and environmental protection. Therefore, the number of companies preparing sustainability reports has increased. However, the communication of sustainability must not be limited to reporting. If it is not done in a transversal and strategic way, there is a risk of losing business, investment, innovation, and competitiveness opportunities. In this scenario, leading companies in sustainability have already begun to act in this sense, integrating environmental and social objectives into their business model and proactively communicating what they do and how they do it to stakeholders. They communicate their actions, their progress, and their goals, as well as their vision. This implies organizations' increasingly greater propensity to prepare non-financial reports to open dialogue with each of their stakeholders and to be ardent in applying the principles of transparency and honesty. It is not only important to believe it, but also to do it and tell it well. Communicating one's sustainability is part of the commitment.

In this environment, the sustainability report assumes a fundamental role and is aimed at representing the impact of the organization's action on stakeholders, society, and the environment. There is a growing trend toward integrated thinking, which combines sustainability with business needs. It is aimed at creating an integrated report with the purpose of documenting the creation of corporate value in a more widely understood form, including its sources, its quality, and its evolution in the short, medium, and long term. In this sense, therefore, it offers a much more articulated representation in terms of the reporting areas involved (strategy and business model, governance, performance, and future prospects) and the resources used to create value.

Integrated reporting has not been adopted by all B Corps in the Italian fashion industry. In fact, some of them prefer to publish their sustainability report separately from their financial ones. As we have discussed in this book, integrated reporting allows stakeholders to appreciate the value generated by organizations and to think of it as shared between society and the environment. In the future, fashion B Corps should adopt more integrated reporting to effectively communicate how they are using financial, human, and social resources in the short, medium, and long term.

Index

Printed in the United States
by Baker & Taylor Publisher Services